The Life Insurance Industry in India

Tapas Kumar Parida • Debashis Acharya

The Life Insurance Industry in India

Current State and Efficiency

palgrave
macmillan

Tapas Kumar Parida
Economic Research Department
State Bank of India,
Corporate Centre
Mumbai, Maharashtra, India

Debashis Acharya
School of Economics
University of Hyderabad,
Central University
Hyderabad, Telangana, India

ISBN 978-981-10-2232-6 ISBN 978-981-10-2233-3 (eBook)
DOI 10.1007/978-981-10-2233-3

Library of Congress Control Number: 2016955695

Printed on acid-free paper

This Palgrave Macmillan imprint is published by Springer Nature
The registered company is Springer Nature Singapore Pte Ltd.
The registered company address is: 152 Beach Road, #22-06/08 Gateway East, Singapore 189721, Singapore

Dedicated to our Teachers…

Preface

The life insurance industry has a long presence in India but the sector opened up for private and foreign participation in August 2000, that is, after the formation of the Insurance Regulatory Development Authority India (IRDAI), with a cap for foreign investment fixed at 26%. With the private and foreign player's participation, the industry structure has moved towards a more competitive market from a pure monopoly. In the post-reform period (2000–2001 to 2014–2015), the insurance sector has recorded an impressive growth, with life insurance business at a compound annual growth rate of 17% in total premium and 21% in new business premium collections. There has also been significant expansion of the customer base, product innovations and operational innovations due to increased competition among the players. However, the insurers still grapple with the issue of profitability. Though the sector has developed in many aspects of insurance, compared to the developed countries like the United States, the United Kingdom and France, the Indian life insurance sector still lags in terms of insurance penetration (ratio of premium volume to gross domestic product) and density (ratio of gross premium volume to total population in a country). Life insurance penetration in India was only 2.72% in 2015 compared to world average of 3.47%. To enhance insurance penetration, the Government of India has passed a number of reforms, including the passing of insurance bill to allow foreign direct investment limit up to 49%. This move may help the insurers to infuse more capital for furthering business in the sector. Thus, it has been more than a decade since the sector was liberalized. The sector merits a thorough review now. In light of this, this book discusses the development and performance of life insurance companies in India by measuring their changing market structure, efficiency and profitability of the life insurance segment in India.

The book aims at a wider audience including students of economics, finance and business, researchers and practitioners in the financial sector. The attempts made in this book to discuss the issues on efficiency after deregulation of the Indian life insurance sector and may motivate different stakeholders to use the results in their respective actions and policies. The stakeholders may also pose new questions to be researched further.

Tapas Kumar Parida
Debashis Acharya

Acknowledgements

The idea for this work originated with a major research project funded by the University Grants Commission in 2010 and awarded to the second author. Later, the first author raised other research questions and addressed them in his PhD thesis. The present wok is a partial outcome of these two pieces. We would like to thank all those friends and institutions that directly and indirectly helped in completing this project. We express our deep sense of gratitude to Prof. Bandi Kamaiah, Dean, School of Economics, and Prof. Ganti Subrahmanyam, Former Director, NIBM, Pune, and visiting professor, School of Economics, University of Hyderabad, for their continuous inspiration during our research. We have learnt a lot from discussions with Prof. Biresh Kumar Sahoo, Xavier Institute of Management Bhubaneswar, on this project. We thank Dr Swayamprava Mishra, presently with the Faculty of Economics, Utkal University, for her research assistance in the initial stages of this work. Several discussions with Mr Satyen Dash, AVP, DFHL PRAMERICA, and Mr Kamalakr Sai, former director of India First Life Insurance, shaped up our thoughts and approach to this work. We thankfully acknowledge the support extended by the University of Hyderabad in numerous ways in the process of writing this book. We appreciate the encouragement and help received from Ms Nupoor Singh and Ms Sagarika Ghosh of Springer Books form the initial stage to completion of the project. We thank the reviewer for the useful comments in improving upon the work. Finally, without the unflinching support of our families, it would have been impossible to write this book.

Contents

About the Authors

Dr Tapas Kumar Parida is an economist with more than 8 years of work experience in macroeconomic research and planning in banks and research organizations, with diversified academic achievement. Presently, he is working as an economist at Economic Research Department of State Bank of India (SBI is the biggest commercial bank in India), Corporate Centre, Mumbai. Prior to joining SBI, he has worked with organizations like Indian Bank, Axis Bank Ltd., Planning Commission, New Delhi, Higher Education Department of Government of Odisha and Xavier Institute of Management Bhubaneswar (XIMB). He is a certified associate of Indian Institute of Banking and Finance (CAIIB) from Indian Institute of Banking and Finance (IIBF), Mumbai, India. He has been awarded a PhD in economics from School of Economics, University of Hyderabad (India). He also holds a master's degree in finance and control (MFC) (which is at par with MBA, Finance) from University of Delhi (India). He writes regularly for a number of magazines and blogs. His publications have appeared in *The Global Banker Magazine*, *Journal of Business Management & Social Sciences Research*, *Insurance Regulatory and Development Authority India (IRDAI) Journal*, the *Insurance Institute of India Journal*, Bima Quest and the *Bank Quest*.

Dr Debashis Acharya is currently a professor in the School of Economics, University of Hyderabad, India. He has been teaching undergraduate and postgraduate courses for the past 18 years. His areas of interest are monetary economics, macroeconomics, and financial economics. Prior to joining University of Hyderabad, he was with the Department of Humanities and Social Sciences, Indian Institute of Technology Madras, Chennai, and Department of Economics, Punjab University, Chandigarh. He has published in the areas of macro-monetary economics and financial economics in national and international refereed journals like *International Journal of Emerging Markets, Economic and Political Weekly, Journal of Economic Studies, European Journal of Operational Research, International Research Journal of Finance and Economics, Banks and Bank Systems, South Asia Economic Journal, Global Journal of Emerging Market Economies* and *Artha Vijanana*.

List of Abbreviations

AIC	Agriculture Insurance Company of India Ltd
AUM	Assets Under Management
CAGR	Compound Annual Growth Rate
CCR	Charnes, Cooper and Rhodes
CD	Cobb–Douglas function
CI	Concentration Indices
CRS	Constant Returns to Scale
DEA	Data Envelopment Analysis
DMUs	Decision Making Units
ECGC	Export Credit Guarantee Corporation of India Limited
EPW	Economic and Political Weekly
FDI	Foreign Direct Investment
FE	Fixed Effects Model
FIPB	Foreign Investment Promotion Board
FIs	Financial Institutions
GCC	Gulf Cooperation Council
GDP	Gross Domestic Product
GDS	Gross Domestic Savings
GIC	General Insurance Corporation
HHI	Herfindahl–Hirschman Index
IAC	Insurance Advisory Committee
IBA	Indian Banks' Association
IPOs	Initial Public Offerings
IRDAI	Insurance Regulatory Development Authority India
IRS	Increasing Returns to Scale
LIC	Life Insurance Corporation
LID	Life Insurance Density

LIP	Life Insurance Penetration
M&As	Mergers and Acquisitions
MES	Minimum Efficient Scale
MPI	Malmquist Productivity Index
NCAER	National Council of Applied Economic Research
OECD	Organisation for Economic Co-operation and Development
OLS	Ordinary Least Squares
PAT	Profit After Tax
PCSE	Panel Corrected Standard Errors
PFRDA	Pension Fund Regulatory and Development Authority
PLI	Postal Life Insurance
PMJDY	Pradhan Mantri Jan Dhan Yojana
PMJJBY	Pradhan Mantri Jeevan Jyoti Bima Yojana
PMSBY	Pradhan Mantri Suraksha Bima Yojana
PTE	Pure Technical Efficiency
RBI	Reserve Bank of India
RE	Random-Effects Model
RoA	Return on Assets
RoE	Return on Equity
RPLI	Rural Postal Life Insurance
SCI	Structural Change Indices
SCP	Structure–Conduct–Performance
SE	Scale Efficiency
SFA	Stochastic Frontier Approach
TE	Technical Efficiency
TFA	Thick Frontier Approach
TFP	Total Factor Productivity
TPA	Third-Party Administrators
ULIPs	Unit Linked Insurance Plan
VAR	Vector Autoregressions
WPI	Wholesale Price Index

List of Figures

List of Tables

CHAPTER 1

Life Insurance in India: Origin, Evolution and the Present State

Abstract This chapter traces the origin of Indian life insurance and discusses its evolution in different phases, distinguishing the pre-liberalization era from the post-liberalization phase. The present state of life insurance in India is discussed in terms of indicators like insurance penetration and density. A comparative picture is drawn with reference to global life insurance. The state of life microinsurance and postal life insurance is briefly discussed followed by the challenges before the future of the industry.

Keywords Insurance penetration · Insurance density · Bancassurance

1.1 Introduction

In the epic *Mahabharata*, Yaksha asked Yudhisthira, 'What is the most wonderful thing in the World'. To this Yudhisthira replied, 'the most wonderful thing in the World is the sight of men watching the dead being carried to burial ground every day and still imagine that, they are eternal' (Life Insurance Compendium 1999–2000). Death is a natural phenomenon and a sublime theme of reflection. Therefore, one should not grieve for what is inevitable and unavoidable, exhorts Lord Shri Krishna in *Shrimad Bhagwad Geeta (the Song Celestial)*. In our worldly life, whenever there is uncertainty there is some element of risk involved. The instinct of seeking protection against such risk is one of the basic motivating forces determining human attitudes. It is believed that the

T.K. Parida, D. Acharya, *The Life Insurance Industry in India*,
DOI 10.1007/978-981-10-2233-3_1

concept of insurance must have originated as a sequel to this instinct. The story of insurance is probably as old as the story of mankind.

Insurance also has a deep-rooted history in India, finding mention in writings of Manu (Manusmriti), Yagnavalkya (Dharmasastra) and Kautilya (Arthashastra). The writings speak of pooling of resources that could be redistributed in times of calamities such as floods, fire, epidemics and famine, etc. This was possibly a precursor to modern-day insurance. In ancient Indian history, the earliest traces of insurance have been preserved in the form of marine trade loans and through carrier's contracts. The Sanskrit term *Yogakshema* (meaning well-being) is found in the Rig Veda and depicts that some kind of commercial insurance was practised by the Aryans in India nearly 3,000 years ago. The Vedic Rishis knew about this and their songs of benevolence contained the term *Yogakshemam*, an idea which has been shaping the Indian thinking since ancient times. Later, the Indian joint family system too fulfilled the need for security to a large extent.

The first plan to form some sort of an insurance organization in India was proposed at the government level. *Sir John Child* (Governor of Bombay, 1681–1690) was instructed by the court of Director of East India Company to constitute an insurance office in the Bombay Island. However, it is not known about the suggestions (Insurance Times 2000).

The rest of the chapter is organized as follows: Section 1.2 discusses the importance of insurance, and Section 1.3 summarizes the meaning, origin, evolution and present state of the Indian life insurance industry. Microinsurance and postal life insurance (PLI) are discussed in Sections 1.4 and 1.5, respectively. In Section 1.6, the trends and progress of the Indian insurance industry with reference to the global market are discussed. Section 1.7 analyses the probable reasons for low penetration and density in India. Finally, Section 1.8 projects a future outlook of the industry, before concluding in Section 1.9.

1.2 Importance of Insurance

A healthy insurance sector is of vital importance to every modern economy. It encourages the savings habit, provides a safety net to rural and urban enterprises and productive individuals, and generates long-term funds for infrastructure development. The insurance industry plays a significant role in India's economy. Insurance is necessary to protect enterprises against risks such as fire and natural disasters. Individuals require insurance services in such areas as health care, life, property and pension. Development of insurance is therefore necessary to support continued economic transformation. Social security and pension reforms also benefit from a mature insurance industry.

In the complex modern world, most importantly life insurance plays a crucial role as risk has increased enormously in every walk of our day to day life. To manage the risk, which can be insured, has led to growth in the life insurance business and evolution of various types of insurance covers. The life insurance products provide a range of financial services to the consumers and provide a major source of investment in the capital market. It provides individuals and the economy with several important financial solutions. First, life insurance products encourage long-term saving and reinvestment of substantial sum in public and private sector projects. By leveraging their role as financial intermediaries, life insurers have become a key source of long-term finance, encouraging development of capital markets. Second, in the phase of growing urbanization, population mobility and formalization of economic relationships between individuals, families and communities, life insurance has taken on increasing importance as a way for individuals and families to manage risk. Third, by pooling risks and smoothing incomes, insurance helps avoid excessive and costly bankruptcies and facilitates lending to businesses. Finally, the availability of insurance enables individuals and entrepreneurs to undertake activities with higher risk and higher return than they would otherwise consider, thus promoting higher productivity and growth (Beck and Webb 2003).

In macroeconomic context, the link between high growth rates and savings is well known from the classical growth theory. In the context of India, a number of studies indicate that a growth rate of 8% is possible, only with a savings rate of 30%. The Table 1.1 specifies the trend of savings starting from 1950–1951 to 2014–2015. It clearly indicates that there is a strong correlation between gross domestic savings (GDS) and gross domestic product (GDP), which stands at 0.99 during the period 1950–1951 and 2014–2015. In literature, it is well argued that a positive relationship exists between saving and insurance premium (Parida and Acharya 2014). So, any study on insurance business needs to look into the other saving activities of the households. The household sector savings include physical and financial saving and account for around 57.8% of the

Table 1.1 Sector-wise domestic savings (Rs. billion)

	FY51	*FY61*	*FY71*	*FY81*	*FY91*	*FY01*	*FY06*	*FY08*	*FY09*	*FY10*	*FY11*	*FY12*	*FY13*	*FY14*	*FY15*
Gross domestic savings (GDS)	10	21	68	266	1,344	5,155	12,352	18,363	18,026	21,823	26,217	30,267	33,648	37,250	41,167
Household savings (HHS)	7	12	45	181	1,086	4,638	8,690	11,183	13,309	16,308	18,002	20,655	22,340	23,609	23,805
Financial savings (FS)	1	5	14	86	496	2,152	4,383	5,802	5,710	7,748	7,739	9,327	10,640	11,694	12,502
Currency	-	-	4	16	63	156	522	813	922	969	1,371	1,062	1,116	1,019	1,317
Bank deposits	-	-	8	56	188	947	2,657	3,890	4,178	3,981	5,483	5,259	5,749	7,742	5,793
Non-banking deposits	-	-	1	4	13	30	5	13	147	185	51	100	172	306	274
Life insurance fund	-	-	2	9	56	339	835	1,698	1,529	2,598	2,101	1,958	1,821	2,052	2,347
Provident and pension fund	-	-	5	21	112	509	620	715	734	1,298	1,411	957	1,240	1,362	2,008
Physical Savings	6	8	32	95	590	2,485	4,307	5,381	7,598	8,560	10,263	13,892	14,637	14,608	13,794
Memo															
GDS % GDP	9.5	11.6	14.3	17.8	22.9	21.9	33.4	36.8	32.0	33.7	33.7	33.8[a]	33.0[a]	32.3[a]	32.3[a]
HHS % GDP	6.5	6.8	9.5	12.1	18.5	19.7	23.5	22.4	23.6	25.2	23.1	22.9	22.1	20.9	19.1
FS % GDP	0.6	2.5	2.9	5.8	8.5	9.1	11.9	11.6	10.1	12.0	9.9	10.4	10.5	10.4	10.0
FS % HHS	9.1	37.2	30.3	47.5	45.7	46.4	50.4	51.9	42.9	47.5	43.0	45.2	47.6	49.5	52.5
Life fund % of FS			15.1	10.6	11.3	15.7	19.0	29.3	26.8	33.5	27.1	21.0	17.1	17.5	18.8

Source: Reserve Bank of India (RBI), MOSPI

[a]As a % gross national disposable income (GNDI)

GDS in 2014–2015 compared to 73% in 2008–2009 and 68.0% in 1950–1951.

In the recent period, 'financial saving' share in household savings has increased to 52.5% in 2014–2015 from 423.0% in 2010–2011. In 2014–2015, the share of financial savings in total household savings increased to 52.5%, which is mainly due to the changes in methodology, following the shift in the base year to 2011–2012 in the calculation of GDP. The 'life fund' accounts around 25% share in 'financial saving' of the household sector and 5% in GDS of India. The 'life fund' share in household financial saving touched the highest 33.5% in 2009–2010 from 10.6% in 1980–1981 but fell to 17.1% in 2012–2013, mainly due to slowdown in the economy, leading to a contraction in premium collections. But, in recent times, it is showing an increasing momentum and is at 18.8% in 2014–2015. There is also a strong correlation of 0.98 between the household financial saving and life fund for the period 1970–1971 to 2014–2015 (Table 1.1).

1.3 Origin and Evolution of the Indian Insurance Industry

Life insurance is a contract between an insurance policyholder and an insurer. The policyholder pays a periodic *premium* or a lump sum and the insurer promises to pay a designated beneficiary, a sum of money (the 'benefits') upon the death of the insured person. Depending on the contract, other events such as terminal illness or critical illness may also entail payment. The life contracts usually fall into two major categories: (1) *protection policies* are designed to provide benefit in case of occurrence of a specified event against a lump sum premium payment. (2) *Investment policies,* on the other hand, facilitate growth of capital by collection of single or regular premiums.

The evolution of Indian insurance can be divided into three phases. The study divides the history of the existence and working of insurance organizations in India into three phases (refer Table 1.2).

1.3.1 Phase I of Life Insurance Evolution

Life insurance in the modern form had its origin in England and made its debut in India in the year 1818, with the establishment of the *Oriental*

Table 1.2 An aggregative view of the Indian insurance industry

Phase I		
Life insurance	1818–1956 (about 138 years)	Many (245) private companies: ***competitive market***
General insurance	1950–1972 (about 122 years)	Many (107) private companies: ***competitive market***
Phase II		
Life insurance	1956–2000 (about 44 years)	Nationalization, public sector ***monopoly***; only one company
General insurance	1972–2000 (about 28 years)	Nationalization, public sector ***monopoly***; one company with four subsidiaries
Phase III		
Life insurance	After 2000	Opened to the entry of private domestic and foreign companies
General insurance		Mixed of public and private companies; ***oligopoly market***

Source: Bhole (2004) and Author's compilation

Life Insurance Company in Calcutta followed by the Bombay Assurance Company in 1823, but the Oriental Insurance company failed in 1834. In 1829, the Madras Equitable had begun transacting life insurance business in the Madras Presidency. These companies were operating in India but did not insure the lives of Indians. Their services were to cater to the needs of the European Community living in India. However, some of the companies later started insurance services for the Indians but they were treated as 'substandard'.[1] In this case, the common adjustment made was a 'rating up' of 5–7 years to normal British Life in India. This meant, treating $p(x)$, the (conditional) probability of dying between x and $x + 1$, for an x-year-old Indian male as if it was $p(x + 5)$ or $p(x + 7)$ of a British male. So, the Indian lives had to pay an ad hoc extra premium of 20% or more. This was a common practice of the European companies at the time whether they are operating in Asia or Latin America. The first company to sell policies to an Indian with 'fair value' was the Bombay Mutual Life Assurance Society that started in 1871.

Due to the failure of a number of insurance companies in India, the British Government enacted the British Insurance Act in 1970. There was an increasing demand to start a state-controlled life insurance company, which the government turned down without any reason. In the last three decades of the nineteenth century, the Bombay Mutual (1871), Oriental (1874) and Empire of India (1897) were started in the Bombay

Presidency. This era, however, was dominated by foreign insurance offices which did good business in India, namely Albert Life Assurance, Royal Insurance, Liverpool and London Globe Insurance, and the Indian offices were up for hard competition from the foreign companies.

The first general insurance company to operate in India was the Triton Insurance Company, established in 1850. This was a British-owned and -operated company. The Indian Mercantile Insurance Company Ltd, established in Bombay 1907, was the first indigenous insurance company. Insurance business was conducted in India without any specific regulation; however, the companies were subject to the Indian Companies Act 1866. In 1912, two sets of regulations were passed: (1) the Indian Life Insurance Companies Act and (2) the Provident Insurance Societies Act. In this legislation, there were a number of remarkable features available; first, this was the first legislation in India that particularly targeted the insurance sector. Second, the legislation left the general insurance business out of it as the government did not feel the necessity to regulate it. Third, they restricted activities of the Indian insurers but not the foreign insurers. After all, the *Insurance Act 1912* provided the first legislation aimed at regulating the insurance companies.

The only significant legislative changes before the insurance Act 1938 was *Act XX of 1928*. It helped the government of India to collect information about (1) Indian insurance companies operating in India, (2) foreign insurance companies operating in India and (3) Indian insurance companies operating in foreign countries. The last two points were missing in the Insurance Act 1912. Thus, the collected information helped to compare the size of the average face value of Indian insurance companies against their foreign counterparts. As per the Indian Insurance Commissioner's report, the average size of the policy sold by Indian companies fell to \$532 in 1938 (\$619 in 1928) compared to \$1,188 (\$1,150 in 1928) for the foreign companies. This was basically due to the robustness and better performance of foreign companies in India (Table 1.3).

By the year 1938, more than 100 insurance companies were doing business in India but the industry was plagued by fraud and mismanagement of funds. In 1937, the government of India set up a consultative committee under the Chairmanship of Mr Sushil C. Sen, a well-known Calcutta solicitor. Finally, the *Insurance Act, 1938* was passed to give order to the industry; it also brought other fundamental changes, including the creation of an insurance wing in the Ministry of Finance. This piece of legislation was the first comprehensive one in India and covered

Table 1.3 Growth of life business in India in pre-nationalization period (1914–1955)

Year	*No. of insurers*	*Of which Indian*[a]	*New business*		*Business in force*		*Life fund*
			No. of policies (000)	*Sum assured (Rs. in crores)*	*No. of policies (000)*	*Sum aassured (Rs. in crores)*	*(Rs. in crores)*
1914	49	36		3.2	–	–	6.36
1915	–	40		2.25	–	–	6.77
1920	–	43	28	5.16	–	–	8.47
1925	–	49	43	8.15	–	–	12.57
1930	68	68	145	27.5	564	124	20.53
1935	–	215	239	43.5	1,095	235	35.19
1940	195	179	206	36.11	1,553	286	62.41
1945	215	198	599	136.3	2,392	557	107.4
1950	209	185	498	139.5	3,280	780	181.5
1955	245	229	831	260.8	4,782	1,220	299.7

Source: Economic and Political Weekly (EPW), privatization and foreign participation in (life) insurance sector, 25 March 2000

[a]Includes Indian insurers and provident societies

both life and general insurance companies. The important legislations include deposits for the life insurance business, supervision of insurance companies, investments, commission of agents and directors appointed by the policyholders among others. However, this act lost its importance after the nationalization of life insurance in 1956 and general insurance in 1972, respectively. With the privatization/deregulation of the sector in the late twentieth century, the Insurance Act 1938 has turned out as the backbone of the current legislation of insurance companies as the Insurance Regulatory and Development Authority of India Act of 1999 was superimposed on the Insurance Act 1938.

1.3.2 Phase II of Life Insurance Evolution

The enactment of the Insurance Act 1938 provided stability to the growing insurance business and the earlier legislations were consolidated and amended to protect the interest of the insuring public. There were a large number of insurance companies, and the level of competition was high.

However, there were also allegations of unfair trade practices. The government of India, therefore, decided to nationalize insurance business. An ordinance was issued on 19 January 1956 nationalizing the life insurance sector and *Life Insurance Corporation* (LIC) came into existence under the introduction of the Life Insurance Act on 1 September 1956. The LIC absorbed 245 Indian and foreign insurers, including 154 Indian, 16 non-Indian insurers and 75 provident societies. By the LIC Act, the government of India has contributed Rs. 5 crores. The then finance minister, Shri C.D. Deshmukh, while piloting the bill, outlined the objectives of LIC (1) to conduct the business with the utmost economy, in a spirit of trusteeship; (2) to charge premium no higher than warranted by strict actuarial considerations; (3) to invest the funds for obtaining maximum yield for the policyholders consistent with safety of the capital; and (4) to render prompt and efficient service to policyholders, thereby making insurance widely popular. Thus, nationalization aimed at overcoming the inefficiency and malpractices involved during the period of private insurance operations, to make life insurance widespread under government control, to restore public confidence and to ensure maximum security to the policyholders' capital. At the same time, nationalization also aimed at using the funds available with LIC for development under the five-year plans.[2]

Further, LIC formulated its objectives in pursuance of recommendations of the Administrative Reforms Commission. Since nationalization, LIC has built up a vast network of 2,048 branches, 100 divisions and 7 zonal offices spread over the country. LIC also transacts business abroad through joint ventures, subsidiaries and also through own offices. LIC plays an important role in the economy for two reasons: (i) as a national insurance agency, it serves to pool and redistribute risks associated with the policyholders in millions of households; and (ii) as a major savings institution, it serves to mobilize a large number of small savings. LIC is a dominant financial intermediary in the economy as it serves to channel investible funds into productive sectors of the economy. These two aspects of LIC together raise a number of issues concerning its present state and future role in the economic development of India. During the period 1956–1999, LIC emerged as a giant financial institution and the sole organization purveying life insurance if we ignore the minimal presence of PLI. The institution succeeded in penetrating many areas and segments of the population and in garnering public money for public welfare.

1.3.2.1 Major Achievements of LIC

The major achievements of the Indian life insurance industry after the nation's independence can be best visualized through the performance of LIC vis-à-vis fulfilment of its objectives. Some of them are outlined next:

- Spread of insurance at a reasonable cost: This was the first and foremost objective of the corporation. At the time of nationalization, the total new business of the 245 erstwhile insurance companies was around Rs. 200 crores of sums assured. Table 2.5 indicates that the business growth numbers are robust as the number of policies increased by 15-fold and the sum assured rose by 194-fold during the period 1957–1998. The individual business in force of the corporation as on 1998 stands at more than 850 lakh policies for a sum assured of over Rs. 4 lakh crores, which can be observed from Tables 1.4 and 1.5.
- Spreading insurance to rural areas: In the pre-nationalization period, life insurance was largely an urban phenomenon. It became the responsibility of the national insurer (LIC) to take insurance to every nook and corner of the country. In 1998, around 51% of the new policies were being sold in the rural areas and the impetus on rural thrust can be further observed from the fact that nearly half of LIC agents were from rural areas and over half of its branches were in village areas.

Table 1.4 LIC's business performance

Year	*Individual new business*			*Individual business in-force*	
	Policies (in lakhs)	*Sum assured (Rs. in crores)*	*First-year premium (Rs. in crores)*	*Policies (in lakhs)*	*Sum assured (Rs. in crores)*
1957[a]	9.3	328.1	13.1	56.9	1,474.0
1969–1970	14.0	1,025.8	41.4	140.4	6,425.0
1979–1980	21.0	2,733.1	134.3	220.9	19,242.6
1989–1990	73.9	23,219.5	1,053.8	404.0	94,823.2
1997–1998	133.1	63,617.7	3,371.5	850.0	400,747.9

Source: Life Insurance Compendium, 1999–2000
[a]16 months

Table 1.5 Rural thrust (individual insurance)

Year	*Policies (in lakhs)*			*Sum assured (Rs. in crores)*		
	Total	*Rural*	*% to total*	*Total*	*Rural*	*% to total*
1960–1961	16.62	5.34	36.53	598.79	182.59	30.49
1969–1970	13.97	4.61	33.00	1,025.80	251.76	24.54
1979–1980	20.96	5.91	28.20	2,733.11	603.77	22.09
1989–1990	73.92	30.48	41.23	23,219.53	8,086.35	34.83
1997–1998	133.11	68.40	51.40	63,617.69	27,550.69	43.00

Source: Life Insurance Compendium, 1999–2000

Table 1.6 LIC's total premium income and life fund

Year	*Total premium (Rs. in crores)*	*Annualized growth (%)*	*Life fund (Rs. in crores)*	*Annualized growth (%)*
1957[a]	88.7		447.8	4.5
1969–1970	260.4	10.9	1,611.0	6.1
1979–1980	875.4	13.0	5,818.1	7.9
1989–1990	4,489.4	30.8	23,471.8	11.1
1997–1998	19,252.1	18.6	105,832.9	12.4
1998–1999	22,805.8	18.5	127,389.1	20.4

Source: Life Insurance Compendium, 1999–2000
[a]16 months

- Mobilizing savings and deployment of the funds to serve the best interest of policyholders and the nation: Another important goal of LIC was to mobilize savings from the different pockets through insurance-linked saving schemes and invest these funds for the planned development of the country. The rate of mobilizing savings increased steadily. In 1957, the total premium income was Rs. 88.7 crores. By 1980, it had grown 10 times, and by 1998, it crossed 200 times (Tables 1.6).
- The steady increase in premium collections has resulted in reservoir of life fund, which has grown from a deficient Rs. 410 crores in 1957 to over Rs. 1,05,832 crores in 1998. In the meanwhile, the extent of contribution of LIC's investments to the nation's planned development is immense (Tables 1.7 and 1.8).

Table 1.7 LIC's investment during five-year plan period

Plan	*Year*	*Investments (Rs. in crores)*
II	1956–1957 to 1960–1961	184
III	1961–1962 to 1965–1966	285
IV	1969–1970 to 1973–1974	1,530
V	1974–1975 to 1978–1979	2,942
VI	1980–1981 to 1984–1985	7,140
VII	1985–1986 to 1989–1990	12,969
VIII	1992–1993 to 1996–1997	56,097
IX	1997–1998 to 2001–2002	19,477

Source: Life Insurance Compendium, 1999–2000

1.3.3 Phase III of Insurance Evolution

The process of reopening of this sector had begun in the early 1990s when the government of India appointed a committee headed by Mr R.N. Malhotra in April 1993 to propose recommendations for reforms in the insurance sector. The committee submitted its report in January 1994 and recommended that the private sector should be permitted to enter the insurance industry. Following the recommendations of the committee, in 1999, the Insurance Regulatory and Development Authority of India (IRDAI) was constituted as an autonomous body to regulate and develop the insurance industry. The IRDAI was incorporated as a statutory body in April 2000. The key objectives of the IRDAI include promotion of competition so as to enhance customer satisfaction through increased consumer choice and lower premiums, while ensuring the financial security of the insurance market.

The IRDAI opened up the market in August 2000 to private players with a foreign investment cap of 26% in equity shareholding. With the private and foreign players' participation, the Indian insurance industry is transforming from a monopoly (2001) to a competitive market structure. As of March 2015, the industry constitutes a total of 53 insurers, of which 24 are in life insurance business (1 public and 23 private) and 28 are in non-life insurance business (6 public; 4 non-life and 2 specialized insurers, namely Export Credit Guarantee Corporation of India Limited (ECGC) and Agriculture Insurance Company of India Limited (AIC), and 22 private, including 17 non-life and 5 stand-alone health insurance[3] companies). In 2013–2014, Cigna TTK Health Insurance Company started its

Table 1.8 LIC's performance at a glance

Year	*1957*	*1969–1970*	*1974–1975*	*1979–1980*	*1995–1996*	*1996–1967*	*1997–1998*	*1998–1999*
Total new business								
Individual (Rs. in crores)	336	990	1,773	2,744	5,208	56,994	63,928	–
Group (Rs. in crores)	–	46	1,340	5,262	62,698	77,559	66,086	76,619
Business in force								
Individual (Rs. in crores)	1,477	6,348	11,852	19,243	295,758	344,619	400,748	–
Group (Rs. in crores)	5	77	1,457	6,137	64,652	64,607	74,799	–
No of polices in force (in lakhs)	57	140	188	221	710	778	850	–
Total no. of lives covered under group (in lakhs)[a]	–	–	23	58	251	245	282	–
Life fund (Rs. in crores)	410	1,611	3,034	5,818	72,780	87,760	105,833	123,789
Investment (Rs. in crores)								
(a) Book value of total investments	382	1,514	2,798	5,748	65,057	82,665	98,948	120,445
(b) Book value of socially oriented investments	–	513	1,219	2,472	50,446	6,107	73,082	88,831
Claims settled number (in lakhs)	–	3	5	7	42	49	57	–
First year (Rs. in crores)	14	42	86	135	2,379	2,877	3,383	4,072
Renewal premium (Rs. in crores)	74	215	412	690	10,771	12,946	15,166	17,710

Source: Life Insurance Compendium, 1999–2000

[a]Including capital redemption and annuity insurance business

Table 1.9 Registered insurers in India

Type of business	*2000*	*2015*[a]		
	Public sector	*Private sector*	*Public sector*	*Total*
1. Life insurance	1	23	1	24
2. Non-life insurance	4	22	6	28
Specialized insurers	1	–	2	2
Health insurance	–	5	–	4
3. Reinsurance	1	–	1	1

Source: IRDAI (2015)
[a]As on 31 March 2015

operation with an equity capital of Rs. 100 crores in the health insurance business segment. In 2000, the total number of insurers in the industry was only six (including LIC, four public-sector general insurers and General Insurance Corporation (GIC) as the national reinsurer) (Table 1.9).

To increase the insurance penetration in the country, the government has taken a number of steps like increase in foreign direct investment (FDI) limit to 49% from 26%, insurance for public at nominal prices (Jan Suraksha) and health insurance schemes for Below Poverty Line (BPL) families, etc. In addition, the IRDAI, the insurance regulator, has allowed insurance companies that have completed 10 years of operation to raise capital through initial public offerings (IPOs). Further, to meet the desired capital and bring efficiency in the four public-sector non-life insurance companies, in the budget 2016–2017, the government has planned to reduce their stakes by registering in the stock exchanges.

1.3.3.1 Life Insurance Performance

Since liberalization, the Indian life insurance industry has gone through two cycles; the first one is characterized by a period of high growth [compound annual growth rate (CAGR) of approximately 31% in new business premium in 2000–2001 to 2010–2011], and the second one is noted as a mere 2% CAGR growth in new business premium for the period 2010–2011 to 2014–2015. Today, LIC is competing with 23 private sector insurers in the industry, who have commenced operations over the period 2000–2015. After the entry of private players in the life insurance business in India, LIC lost its market share from 100% in FY01 to 69.8% in FY11; however, interestingly in the last three years, LIC gained market share and reached 75.5% in FY14 but declined in FY15 to 73.0% (Table 1.10).

Table 1.10 Business performance of life insurance sector

Particulars	*2000–2001*	*2001–2002*	*2005–2006*	*2010–2011*	*2011–2012*	*2012–2013*	*2013–2014*	*2014–2015*
No. of insurers	5	12	15	23	24	24	24	24
No. of branch offices	2,199	2,306	3,865	11,546	11,167	10,285	11,032	11,033
Number of new policies issued (in lakhs)		253.7	354.6	481.5	441.9	441.9	408.7	259.08
1-Year premium (including single premium in Rs. crores)	9,707	19,857	38,786	126,381	113,942	107,361	120,320	113,143
% growth		104.56	47.93	15.01	–9.85	–5.78	12.1	–5.9
Total premium (Rs. in crores)	34,898	50,094	105,876	291,605	287,072	287,203	314,283	328,101
% growth		43.54	27.78	9.85	–1.57	0.05	9.4	4.4
LIC market share (on total premium)	99.98	99.46	85.75	69.78	70.68	72.70	75.39	73.00
Individual business in force (no of policies) (in '000)	–	–	193,601	329,187	335,284	336,112	–	–
Individual business in force (sum assured) (Rs. in crores)	–	–	1,554,045	3,856,219	4,311,470	4,719,832	–	–
No. of individual agents (nos.)	–	476,902	1,423,839	2,639,392	2,358,885	2,122,757	2,188,500	2,067,907
Commission expense ratio (total premium)[a]	–	–	–	6.29	6.46	6.71	6.63	5.93
Life fund (Rs. in crores)	194,010	230,369	397,189	841,075	974,620	1,120,000	1,288,225	1,495,309
PAT (Rs. in crores)	291	594	–452	2,657	5,974	6,948	7,588	7,611

Source: IRDAI (2015)

[a]Is the ratio between commission expenses and the premium underwritten by life insurers

PAT: profit after tax

In 2014–2015, out of the 23 private life insurers, 6 companies in total premium and in first-year premium (including single premium) registered a negative growth. However, on a positive note, on a cumulative basis both LIC and private insurers together have covered 95.16% of all districts in the country. The number of districts with no presence of life insurance offices stood at 31 in the country. Out of these, 23 districts belong to six of the northeastern states, namely Arunachal Pradesh, Assam, Nagaland, Manipur, Mizoram and Sikkim. At the end of March 2015, all the 24 life insurers complied with the stipulated requirement of solvency ratio of 1.5 (LIC: 1.55).

1.3.3.2 Channels of Distribution

The new insurers have contributed to the sector's development significantly by enhancing product awareness, promoting consumer education and information and creating more organized distribution channels like agency, bancassurance, broking, direct and corporate agency, amongst others. The development of bancassurance channel has helped the private sector players to break into the market quickly and gain market share. In 9 years (2006–2007 to 2014–2015) of 'bancassurance' in India, the life insurance premium (both individual and group) collection by banks registered a CAGR growth of 16.9% compared to 5.2% growth in total life premium through all other channels. The 'Corporate agents – banks' channel accounts for about 11.3% share in new business life insurance (individual) for 2014–2015 compared to 4.9% share in 2006–2007. The decline in share by the 'Corporate agents – banks' channel in 2013–2014 can be attributed to policy uncertainty regarding bancassurance in the country. Though this channel is gaining importance in India, it still remains low as compared to the developed markets (Spain 65%, France 60%, Belgium 50%, the United Kingdom 16%, China 56%, Brazil 50%, South Korea 37% and Taiwan 63%) (Table 1.11).

1.3.3.3 Issues in Bancassurance Model in India

In the Union Budget speech of 2013–2014, the finance minister permitted banks to act as insurance brokers for better insurance penetration and to reduce misselling of insurance products by existing agents. As brokers, banks, apart from being able to give customers products of multiple insurers, would also be responsible for the sale of that product because of the

Table 1.11 Channel-wise new business performance of life insurers in individual policies segment (% share)

Channels	*FY07*	*FY08*	*FY09*	*FY10*	*FY11*	*FY12*	*FY13*	*FY14*	*FY15*
Individual agents	72.2	72.2	65.5	60.9	53.9	46.6	46.4	40.6	36.4
Corporate agents – banks	4.9	7.3	8.4	8.5	9.8	11.3	11.3	9.4	11.3
Corporate agents – others	2.4	3.7	4.0	3.6	2.6	2.0	1.5	1.0	1.3
Brokers	0.5	0.6	1.0	1.3	1.3	1.3	1.2	1.1	1.3
Direct selling	18.3	16.2	21.1	25.7	32.4	38.8	39.5	47.8	49.7
MI agents	0.0	0.0	0.0	0.0	0.0	0.0	0.0	0.0	0.0
Common service centres (CSCs)	0.0	0.0	0.0	0.0	0.0	0.0	0.0	0.0	0.0
Total	100.0	100.0	100.0	100.0	100.0	100.0	100.0	100.0	100.0

MI: Malmquist index.
Source: IRDAI (2015)

fiduciary responsibility they would shoulder as brokers. However, as agents they always represent the interest of the insurer and not that of the policy-holder. Consequently, Reserve Bank of India (RBI) and IRDAI have issued guidelines on insurance broking norms. The move definitely will help in expanding the insurance distribution base and enable banks to boost their fee-based income. The new guidelines also propose to avoid any conflict of interest – for instance, banks undertaking insurance broking business will not be allowed to enter into agreements either for corporate agency or for referral arrangements for insurance, either departmentally or through subsidiaries/group companies. In a paper by Parida (2014), it has been shown that banks are more comfortable with corporate agency arrangements and are resistant to take additional risk on insurance broking. The main reasons are noted next:

- On an average, less than 2% of a bank's profit comes from selling insurance policies. So, if one accounts for the cost involved for banks to set-up separate departments and train their staff for insurance broking, it does not seem a viable option. Also under the broking business, banks would earn less commission (30% of first-year premium and 5% on renewal for selling a life insurance policy) as compared to corporate agency model (commission 40% of first-year premium and 7.5% on renewal for selling a life insurance policy). So, this may not motivate the banks to go for broker model with high risk and low return.
- There is a cap on business from one client (50%) and on business from the promoter group (insurance company) at 25%. This does seem prudent from a risk management point of view, it also militates against common sense from another angle. But the issue is, 'Why would a company put in so much capital and effort in order to see the bank branches sell just 25% of its products while it can earn 75% of income from its competitor's products?' However, there are many big banks that are already doing insurance business through subsidiary route. The caps on business may work as a disincentive for banks to apply for insurance broking licence.
- Besides, for banks and insurance companies, there are also issues of technology investments and training of workforce. Even integrating an insurance company's system with a bank's core banking system can take months and is often riddled with hiccups. So, the difficulties of doing that with four or five companies would increase the

operational cost to manifold (training, department set-up, regular reporting and scrutiny and system integrations, etc.).

- Finally, research suggests that some of the products of insurance, especially from the long-term savings point of view, closely resemble term deposits of banks, so there are apprehensions that insurance products would supplant bank products instead of supplementing them. However, if the commission is more than the return on deposits, then banks would be motivated to adopt insurance business as one of their key areas of operations.

1.4 Microinsurance in India

Microinsurance regulations issued by the IRDAI have provided a fillip in propagating microinsurance as a conceptual issue. With the positive and facilitative approach adopted under the microinsurance regulations, it is expected that all insurance companies would come out with a progressive business approach and carry forward the spirit of regulations, thereby extending insurance penetration to all segments of society.

The number of microinsurance agents at the end of March 2015 stood at 20,855, of which 19,379 agents are those belonging to LIC and the remaining are from the private sector insurance companies. In micro-insurance life, the individual new business premium in 2014–2015 was Rs. 28.9 crores for 8.16 lakh policies and the group business amounted to Rs. 215.60 crore premium for 2.31 crore lives.

1.5 Evolution and Progress of PLI in India

1.5.1 Postal Life Insurance

PLI was introduced on 01 February 1884 with the express approval of the Secretary of State (for India) to Her Majesty, the Queen Empress of India. It was essentially a scheme of state insurance mooted by the then director-general of post offices, Mr F.R. Hogg, in 1881 as a welfare scheme for the benefit of postal employees and was later extended to the employees of the Telegraph Department in 1888. In 1894, PLI extended insurance cover to female employees of P&T Department at a time when no other insurance company covered female lives. It is the oldest life insurer in this country. PLI is an exempted insurer under Section 118(c) of the Insurance Act of 1938. It is also exempted under Section 44(d) of LIC Act, 1956.

Initially, the upper limit of life insurance was only Rs. 4,000 which has now been increased to Rs. 10 lakhs for all schemes combined – endowment assurance and whole life assurance. Over the years, PLI has grown substantially from a few hundred policies in 1884 to 64 lakh policies as on 31 March 2015. It now covers employees of central and state governments, central and state public-sector undertakings, universities, government-aided educational institutions, nationalized banks, local bodies, etc. PLI also extends the facility of insurance to the officers and staff of the defence services and paramilitary forces. Apart from single insurance policies, PLI also manages a group insurance scheme for the extra departmental employees (Gramin Dak Sevaks) of the Department of Posts (Table 1.12).

However, PLI is not for investors who are looking for new-age products like unit-linked insurance policies (ULIPs) and pension plans. The postal department offers six plain vanilla plans, namely Suraksha (whole life assurance), Santosh (endowment assurance), Suvidha (convertible whole life insurance), Sumangal (anticipated endowment assurance), Yugal Suraksha (joint endowment) and Children's Policy. These policies just offer death cover while LIC and other insurance companies offer accidental death benefit with extra premiums.

1.5.2 Rural Postal Life Insurance

Rural postal life insurance (RPLI) came into being as a sequel to the recommendations of the Malhotra Committee for Reforms in the Insurance Sector. The committee had observed in 1993 that only 22% of the insurable population in this country has been insured; life insurance funds accounted for only 10% of the gross household savings. The committee also observed that the 'Rural Branch Postmasters who enjoy a position of trust in the community have the capacity to canvass life insurance business within their respective areas'.

The government accepted the recommendations of Malhotra Committee and allowed PLI to extend its coverage to the rural areas to transact life insurance business with effect from 24 March 1995, mainly because of the vast network of post offices in the rural areas and low cost of operations. The prime objective of the scheme is to provide insurance cover to the rural public, in general, and to benefit weaker sections and women workers of rural areas, in particular, and also to spread insurance awareness among the rural population. The growth of the RPLI is satisfactory over the years, as shown in Table 1.13.

Table 1.12 Postal life insurance (PLI) (amount in Rs. crores)

Year	*No. of policies in force*	*% growth*	*Premium income*	*% growth*	*Sum assured amount*	*% growth*	*Corpus of fund*	*% growth*
2001–2002	20,08,575	–	502	13.2	11,870	–	5,090	–
2002–2003	20,98,577	4.5	591	17.7	13,677	15.2	5,797	13.9
2003–2004	22,08,683	5.2	698	18.2	15,918	16.4	6,620	14.2
2004–2005	28,57,797	29.4	905	29.6	18,747	17.8	7,678	16.0
2005–2006	30,98,248	8.4	1,079	19.2	22,952	22.4	8,934	16.4
2006–2007	32,97,825	6.4	1,212	12.3	26,753	16.6	10,343	15.8
2007–2008	35,50,084	7.7	1,480	22.2	31,469	17.6	12,082	16.8
2008–2009	38,41,539	8.2	1,861	25.7	38,403	22.0	14,153	17.1
2009–2010	42,83,302	11.5	2,413	29.7	51,210	33.3	16,656	17.7
2010–2011	46,86,245	9.4	3,003	24.5	64,078	25.1	19,802	18.9
2011–2012	50,06,060	6.8	3,681	22.6	76,591	19.5	23,011	16.2
2012–2013	52,19,326	4.3	4,557	23.8	88,896	16.1	28,190	22.5
2013–2014	54,06,093	3.6	5,352	17.4	1,02,276	15.1	32,716	16.1
2014–2015	64,61,413	19.5	–	–	1,30,745	27.83	37,571	14.8

Source: Directorate, PLI, Department of Post

Table 1.13 Rural postal life insurance (RPLI) (amount in Rs. crores)

Year	*No. of policies in force*	*% growth*	*Premium income*	*% growth*	*Sum assured*	*% growth*	*Corpus of fund*	*% growth*
2001–2002	11,33,013	–	95	39.8	4,404	–	341	–
2002–2003	17,95,070	58.4	171	80.9	7,465	69.5	511	49.7
2003–2004	26,66,485	48.5	245	43.2	12,385	65.9	756	48.1
2004–2005	37,96,773	42.4	38,087	55.3	18,896	52.6	1,128	49.1
2005–2006	47,02,776	23.9	475	24.7	25,230	33.5	1,625	44.1
2006–2007	52,46,673	11.6	601	26.5	33,866	34.2	2,285	40.6
2007–2008	61,67,928	17.6	665	10.6	41,846	23.6	3,004	31.5
2008–2009	73,56,446	19.3	879	32.3	53,072	26.8	3,994	33.0
2009–2010	99,25,103	34.9	1,357	54.4	59,573	12.2	5,525	38.3
2010–2011	1,22,03,345	23.0	1,111	–18.1	66,132	11.0	6,608	19.6
2011–2012	1,35,47,355	11.0	1,559	40.3	69,754	5.5	9,141	38.3
2012–2013	1,46,64,650	8.3	1,703	9.3	75,154	7.7	11,388	24.6
2013–2014	1,50,14,314	2.4	1,960	15.1	79,466	5.7	13,352	17.5
2014–2015	2,35,14,055	56.6	–	–	1,05,204	132.4	14,968	112.1

Source: Directorate, PLI, Department of Post

1.6 Life Insurance Scenario: India Versus World

1.6.1 Global Life Insurance Scenario

The insurance industry has faced another challenging year in 2015, with a moderate economic growth and low interest rates. Despite the challenges, the global insurance industry grew by 3.8% in 2015 compared to 3.5% in 2014. However, in nominal US$ terms, premiums were down by 4.2% due to widespread currency depreciation against the US$. In real terms, life premium growth slowed to 4% from a 4.3% gain in 2014 (2015: US$ 2,534 billion). In advanced markets, life premiums grew 2.5%, down from 3.8% growth the previous year. North America returned to positive growth after two years of decline. Life premium growth was also stronger in advanced Asia, driven by Japan and Korea. In Western Europe, however, growth slowed significantly. In the emerging markets, overall life premium growth almost doubled to near 12%, supported by strong sector performance in emerging Asia. Growth also improved in Latin America but was slower in the Middle East and Central Asia, and Africa. In Central and Eastern Europe (CEE), premiums contracted. Last year, life premium growth fell short of the pre-crisis average in advanced markets yet again, but it was slightly higher in the emerging markets.

Despite the above-average growth rates in 2014 and 2015, life insurance premiums have been sluggish since the financial crisis in 2008. On average, advanced market premiums have stagnated since then, with very little and even negative life premium growth in Western Europe and North America. The emerging markets have also slowed markedly, with premium growth less than half pre-crisis levels (Figs. 1.1 and 1.2).

Life premiums are expected to grow in both the advanced and emerging markets in 2016. Growth is forecast to accelerate slightly in the advanced but decelerate in the emerging countries. The small improvement in the advanced markets will come from an expected recovery in Oceania and modest acceleration in Western Europe. In North America, growth will remain roughly stable. In the emerging markets, the pace of growth reflects sustained strong performance in emerging Asia. Premium growth in China, though slowing, is expected to remain strong in 2016. The fast-growing sharia compliant/takaful business in Indonesia and Malaysia is expected to further benefit the life sector. In contrast, growth in Latin America will remain below

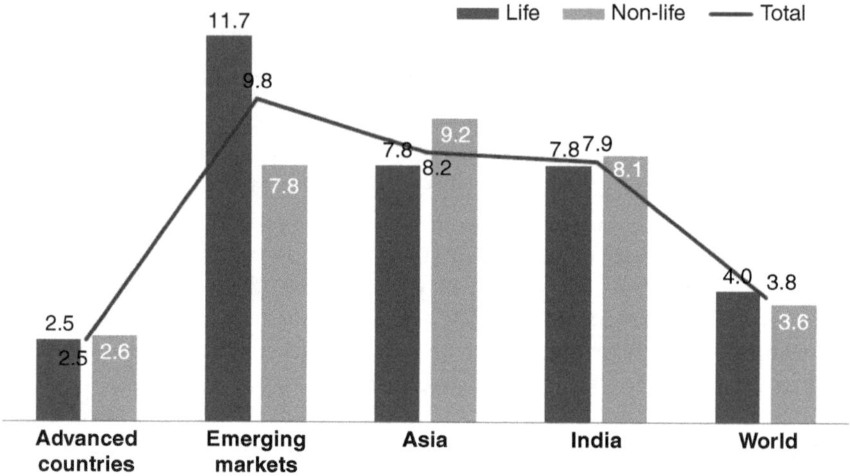

Fig. 1.1 Real premium growth rate in 2015
Source: Sigma 3/2016, Swiss Re

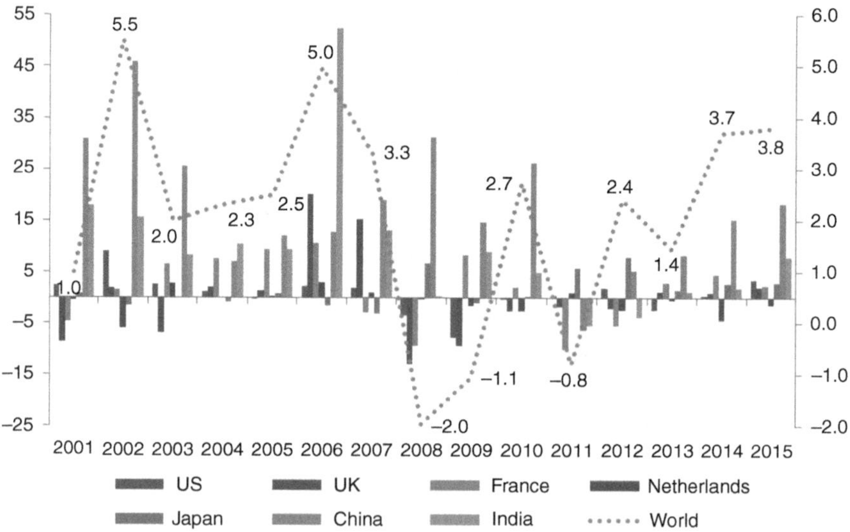

Fig. 1.2 Real premium growth rate: cross-country
Source: Sigma, Swiss Re

recent trend levels due to price competition, demand weakness and heightened financial and economic volatility. Life premiums will also remain under pressure in most European Union (EU) countries and are expected to decline in Russia due to the ongoing economic difficulties there. In Africa, life insurance penetration is still very low, so there is ample potential for growth (Sigma 3/2016).

Interest rates and the macroeconomic and financial market environment will continue to shape the outlook for the primary life insurance industry. Downside risks from just modest global economic growth, persistently low interest rates, volatility in the financial markets and regulatory changes remain significant in the short and medium term. With profitability under pressure, life insurers will continue to focus on improving capital management, lowering expenses and enhancing investment yields.

1.6.2 Indian Insurance in Global Scenario

In global insurance market, India ranked 15th in total premium in 2014 (life rank: 11th; non-life rank: 20th) among 88 countries. During 2001–2014, India's share in the global insurance market improved to 1.46% in total premium (life: 2.08%; non-life: 0.69%) in 2014 from 0.4% (life: 0.7%; non-life: 0.3%) in 2001. Figure 1.3 indicates that there is a continuous improvement in India's market share in the global insurance industry till 2010; however, it declined thereafter due to contraction in new business premium collections in the country. In 2014–2015, the trend reverted and is showing an upward trend.

1.6.3 Insurance Penetration and Density in India

In the global market, insurance penetration[4] and density[5] is universally accepted as a measure of the performance and development of the insurance sector. In comparison with other countries in the world (refer Table 2.2), India's insurance penetration was at a very low level of 3.4% (life: 2.7%; non-life: 0.7%) in 2015, which is much lower than the world average of 6.23% (life: 3.47%; non-life: 2.77%). Although the penetration of Indian insurance is higher than that of some South Asian countries like Pakistan (0.71%) and Sri Lanka (1.15%), however, it lags behind other developed countries like the United States (7.29%), the

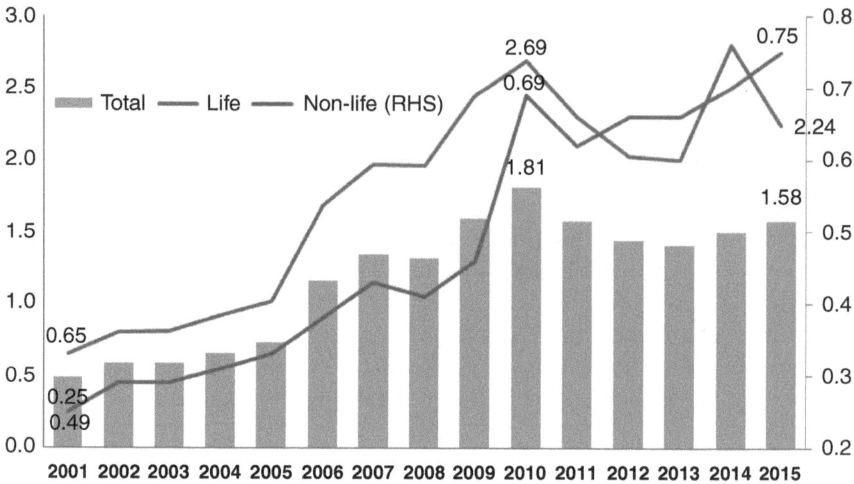

Fig. 1.3 India's progress in insurance business in the world (% share)

Source: Sigma, Swiss Re

United Kingdom (9.97%) and Asian countries like Japan (10.82%), South Korea (11.42%) and Singapore (7.25%). Further, India's insurance density was also at a very low level of $54.7 in 2015 (life: $43.2; non-life: $11.5) compared with world average of $621.2 (life: $345.7; non-life: $275.6) (Table 1.14).

As shown in Fig. 1.4, the trend line of insurance penetration indicates that India's insurance penetration had consistently gone up from 2.7% in 2001 (life: 2.2%; non-life: 0.6%) to 5.2% (life: 4.6%; non-life: 0.6%) in 2009, before it fell to 3.3% (life: 2.6%; non-life: 0.7%) in 2014. Again, due to Jan Suraksha measures by the government of India, the insurance penetration was showing an upward movement and was at 3.4% (life: 2.7%; non-life: 0.7%) in 2015.

The second indicator, that is, insurance density, indicates a consistent rise up to the year 2009 and fall thereafter (refer Fig. 1.5). The life insurance density in India had gone up from $11.5 (life: $9.1; non-life: $2.4) in 2001 to $54.7 (life: $43.2; non-life: $11.5) in 2015, though it reached the peak of $64.4 (life: $55.7; non-life: $8.7) in 2010.

Table 1.14 Cross-country comparison of insurance penetration and density (2015)

Country	*Insurance density (US$)*			*Insurance penetration (%)*		
	Life	*Non-life*	*Total*	*Life*	*Non-life*	*Total*
USA	1,719.2	2,376.6	4,095.8	3.05	4.22	7.28
UK	3,291.8	1,066.7	4,358.5	7.53	2.44	9.97
France	2,263.0	1,129.0	3,392.0	6.20	3.09	9.29
South Africa	687.9	154.6	842.5	12.0	2.7	14.69
Switzerland	4,078.6	3,291.7	7,370.3	5.1	4.12	9.22
Japan	2,717.0	836.8	3,553.8	8.27	2.55	10.82
India	43.2	11.5	54.7	2.72	0.72	3.44
China	153.1	127.6	280.7	1.95	1.63	3.57
Singapore	2,931.5	893.7	3,825.1	5.55	1.69	7.25
South Korea	1,939.9	1,094.3	3,034.2	7.30	4.12	11.42
World	345.7	275.6	621.2	3.47	2.77	6.23

Source: Swiss Re, Sigma 3/2016

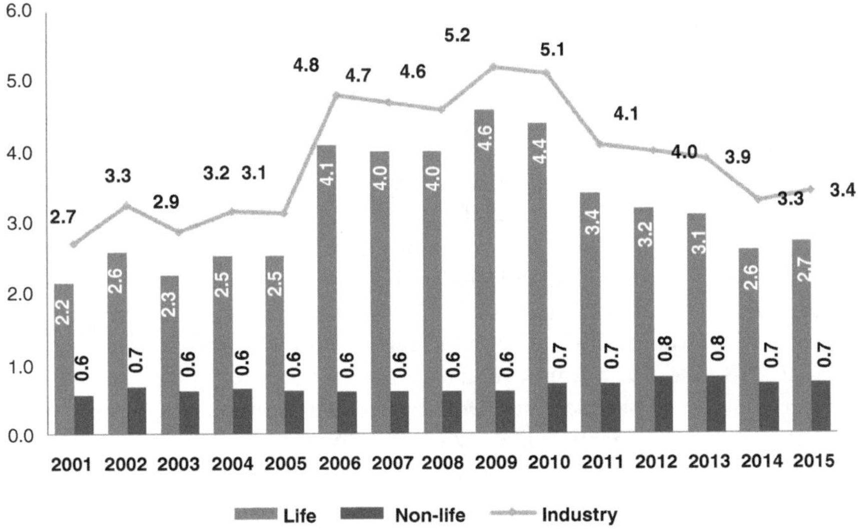

Fig. 1.4 Insurance penetration in India (% GDP)

Source: Sigma 3/2016, Swiss Re

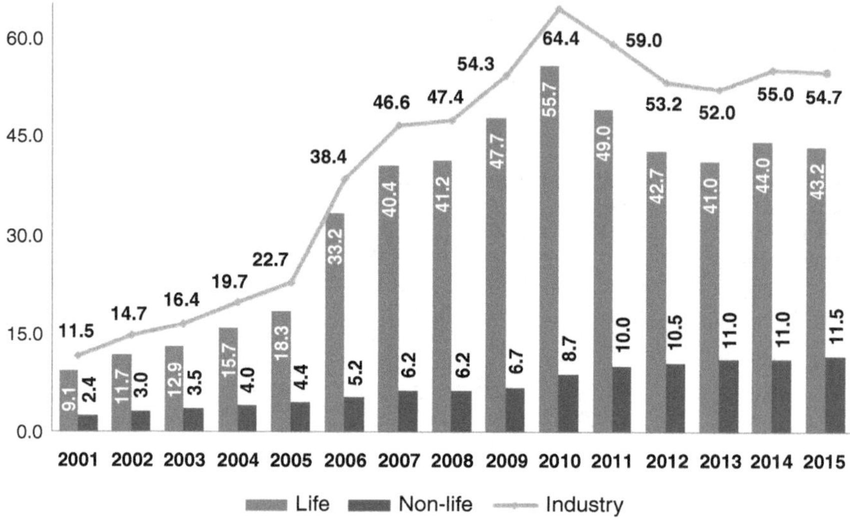

Fig. 1.5 Insurance density in India (US$)
Source: Sigma, Swiss Re

1.7 Reasons of Low Insurance Penetration and Density in India

Prior to deregulation of the sector, it was perceived that the low level of insurance penetration was mainly due to ineffective market strategies adopted by the insurers. The advertising initiatives were limited to only print and electronic media, which mainly promoted life insurance products as tax-saving tools for individuals. However, in the post-deregulation period, the level of insurance penetration and density in the country increased but still at a low level as compared to other countries like the United States, the United Kingdom, France and South Africa. This may be due to a number of factors like economic slowdown, population rise and slowdown in premium collections.

In a survey report, the National Council of Applied Economic Research (NCAER)[6] (2011) found that apart from macroeconomic issues the insurance penetration in India is low due to a number of other factors like low consumer preference, untapped rural markets and constrained distribution channels. In urban areas, life insurance penetration is approximately 65%

and is considerably lesser in the low-income unbanked urban areas. The life insurance penetration in the banked rural segment is estimated to be approximately 40% and negligible in the unbanked rural areas. According to feedback received in the survey, the problem has been exacerbated due to (1) agents' inability to clearly explain the features of the products, (2) lengthy documents that are not user-friendly and (3) the perception that agents are only concerned with their commissions.

1.8 Challenges, Opportunities and Future Outlook

The Indian insurance industry is now facing a wave of structural change generated by shifting macroeconomic and demographic conditions, demand for new products and services, and increasing regulatory pressure, which may put a number of insurers to confront new and far-reaching challenges to remain successful in their business operations. However, the emerging economic environment also presents exciting opportunities for those insurers who aspire to recognize and are able to adapt it. The key to success for the companies that are committed to grab a greater pie in the Indian insurance market will be greater focus on (1) achieving cost efficiency, (2) data analytics and (3) product innovation with lower premium, which is needed to create growth and competitive advantage.

1.8.1 Challenges

At present, the insurance companies face difficulty in building their brand image. Convincing customers who are not comparatively well informed about the intangible benefits of life insurance is indeed an enormous task for the insurance companies. The next major difficulty faced by the insurance companies relates to setting up infrastructure and reaching out to as many areas as possible. Further, there is a need for innovating or customizing new products to meet the changing demands of the people. Managing the funds also remains a challenge.

In terms of regulation, the challenges are for the government and the IRDAI as there are 53 insurers, thousands of agents, brokers and intermediaries. The trade-off between excessive control due to regulation and certain degree of autonomy has a bearing on the industry's growth. To regulate the sector, the IRDAI, given its regulatory reach and qualified personnel, seems to be well equipped to embark on the task of overseeing the sector. There is also a proposal to form a federation of insurance companies similar to the Indian Banks' Association (IBA), which will provide clear principles, lay down a code of insurance ethics and generally act as a facilitator for both the life and non-life industry with the government and regulator.

1.8.2 Opportunities

The population in India is indeed vast, and the existing dominant player LIC has managed to cover only 5% of the total population of the country. Further, in India, the ratio of assets of insurance companies to those of banks is around 3% while the ratio in the United States is 10%. This serves as another indicator of the potential that the industry can go forward to tap the vast market available in the country.

Going forward, the IRDAI will play a key role in laying down the ground rules and paving the way for the sector's growth and development. In addition, the sector will be next only to the banking industry in creating employment opportunities in the country. Further, a number of web portals and financial magazines are exclusively devoted to insurance and also a few training institutes are being set up to create awareness of insurance in the country. Many of the universities and management institutes have already introduced courses on insurance to educate the technicalities of the insurance business, which will help students to make a career in insurance. Additionally, the Indian pension market is at a nascent stage and is expected to witness a sea change in the coming years with huge expansion in terms of premium and number of policies. Finally, health insurance is likely to get a boost from the government with a separate tax deduction under 80C, which ultimately will push improvement in the quality of medical treatment and facilities in the country.

1.8.3 Future Prospects

The future of India's insurance sector looks bright as the country has a favourable demographics, growing awareness and investment-friendly government. The government and regulator (IRDAI) are constantly looking to increase awareness among the people, liberalizing policies to attract foreign investment and tax benefits to customer, etc., to give businesses the best possible environment to grow. It is estimated by

Boston Consulting Group (BCG) that India's insurable population may touch 75 crores by 2020, with life expectancy at 74 years. In addition, life insurance is projected to comprise 35% of total financial savings by the end of this decade from 18.7% in 2014–2015. Improving consumer sentiment and financial market conditions will also support demand for unit-linked and pension products in India.

Finally, to predict the future of Indian insurers turning global players, this would be too early to address as the Indian industry holds only 1.58% (Swiss Re 2016) of the global market. We expect the industry will consolidate its position in the domestic market before venturing abroad.

1.9 Concluding Remarks

The Indian insurance industry has always been an attractive market for global insurers to expand their business, mainly due to the demographic profile and untapped business opportunities. However, the FDI limit for insurance in India is the lowest globally. China, Indonesia and Malaysia have an FDI limit of 50%, 80% and 51%, respectively. Japan, South Korea, Vietnam, Hong Kong and Taiwan allow 100% FDI. In this context, the government's move to increase the FDI limit in insurance to 49% is a welcome move, which aims at the global investors and is expected to bring in the much required foreign capital to meet the needs of the industry. This may help the insurers to expand their footprint to support the government's objective of financial inclusion in the country.

Notes

1. Substandard in insurance parlance refers to lives with physical disability.
2. In 1974, as a follow-up to the recommendations suggested by the Administrative Reforms Committee, appointed by the government of India, LIC explicitly aimed at bringing all possible sections of the society under life insurance by making it cheaply available, maintaining it economically and increasing the productivity of the personnel.
3. Namely Star Health & Allied Insurance Company, Apollo Munich Health Insurance Company, Max Bupa Health Insurance Company, Religare Health Insurance Company and Cigna TTK Health Insurance Company.
4. Insurance penetration is measured as ratio of premium (in US$) to GDP (in US$).

5. Insurance density is measured as ratio of premium (in US$) to total population.
6. Pre-Launch Survey Report of Insurance Awareness Campaign by NCAER in 2011; funded by IRDAI.

References

Beck, T., and Webb, I. (2003), "Economic, Demographic, and Institutional Determinants of Life Insurance Consumption across Countries", *The World Bank Economic Review*, Vol. 17, Issue 1, pp. 51–88.

Bhole, L. M. (2004), "*Financial Institutions and Markets: Structure, Growth and Innovations*", 4th Edition Book. New Delhi: Tata McGraw-Hill Education.

Insurance Times. (2000), "*Life Insurance Compendium", 1999–2000"*. Insurance Times, Kolkata.

IRDAI (2015), *Annual Reports and Hand Book on Indian Insurance Statistics.* Hyderabad: Insurance Regulatory and Development Authority of India (IRDAI).

Karunagaran, A. (2006), "Bancassurance: A Feasible Strategy for Banks in India?", *Reserve Bank of India Occasional Papers*, Vol. 27, Issue 3, pp. 125–162 (Winter 2006).

NCAER. (2011), "Pre-Launch Survey Report of Insurance Awareness Campaign", *National Council of Applied Economic Research, 2011*, Sponsored by IRDAI, Hyderabad.

Parida, T. K. (2014), "Banking with Insurance in India: Agency or Broker", *The Journal of Insurance Regulatory and Development Authority of India (IRDAI), Hyderabad*, Vol. XII, Issue 4, pp. 20–22 (April 2014).

Parida, T. K., & Acharya, D. (2014), "Life Insurance Demand in India: Some Empirical Observations", *The Journal of Insurance Institute of India*, Vol. II, Issue II (October–December 2014), 129–134.

Reserve Bank of India. (2015), "*Handbook of Statistics on Indian Economy 2014–15*". RBI, Mumbai.

Swiss *Re*. (2016), "Global Insurance in 2015", *Sigma*, March 2016.

CHAPTER 2

Analysing the Technical Efficiency and Productivity Change of Life Insurance Companies in India

Abstract This chapter analyses technical efficiency of the Indian life insurance industry comprising 13 life insurance companies for the period 2002–2003 to 2014–2015. Data envelopment analysis (DEA) is employed to measure technical efficiency, and Malmquist productivity index is used to measure productivity change. The results imply that deregulatory efforts might have had only marginal effect on productivity and efficiency of the Indian life insurance industry.

Keywords Efficiency · Technical efficiency · Scale efficiency · Productivity

2.1 Introduction

Efficiency has become a buzz word in financial market, in general, and in banking and insurance, in particular. Researchers around the world have explored and probed every aspect of efficiency and a substantial research effort has gone into measuring the efficiency of financial institutions (FIs). Efficiency measurement has captured a great deal of attention not only in services industries like insurance and banking, but also in industries like manufacturing, mining, etc. The measurement of efficiency of insurers serves two important purposes: first, it helps to benchmark the relative efficiency of an individual insurer against the 'best practice' insurer(s); and second, it helps to evaluate the impact of various policy measures on the efficiency and performance of these institutions. However, efficiency

T.K. Parida, D. Acharya, *The Life Insurance Industry in India*,
DOI 10.1007/978-981-10-2233-3_2

measurement in insurance is not straightforward due to difficulty in defining the inputs and outputs of an insurer. Further, the insurance companies are not homogeneous with respect to the types of products they offer. There is also question of various concepts of efficiency that can be employed to compute relative efficiency scores of individual insurers.

In India, prior to liberalization, the policymakers have recognized that inefficiency is an important factor for the high cost of insurance services and low penetration in the country. So, the sector was liberalized in 2000 to enhance operational efficiency of the sector as a whole as well as of individual insurers. It has been a decade and half since liberalization of the sector warranting an in-depth analysis of the efficiency of the industry. Such an exercise on efficiency to judge the industry's performance seems to be absent to the best of our knowledge. This chapter evaluates the efficiency of life insurance companies and examines the productivity change of these companies by using data envelopment analysis (DEA) and Malmquist Productivity Index (MPI) for the period 2002–2003 to 2014–2015.

The rest of the chapter is organized into five sections. Section 2 discusses the relevant literature on insurance efficiency. Section 3 presents the methodology and data description. The empirical results are discussed in Section 4. Finally, Section 6 concludes with a brief summary.

2.2 Review of Literature

In this section, a review, though not exhaustive, of some of the major past studies is being attempted and the research issues are highlighted.

2.2.1 International Studies

Efficiency comparisons at the international level have received significant attention in the insurance literature. Weiss and Cummins (1991) is probably the first cross-country comparison of efficiency and the study provides (bilateral) divisia and multilateral divisia indexes of output, input and productivity for the property-liability (P-L) insurance industry for countries such as the United States, West Germany, Switzerland, France and Japan. The time period studied is 1975–1987. The results indicate that considerable diversity exists among different countries, with Japan showing the weakest productivity growth. The United States and West Germany are associated overall with high productivity.

In another paper, Rai (1996) examines the cost efficiency of insurance firms in 11 countries over a 5-year period of 1988–1992. Two x-inefficiency measures are derived, one from the stochastic cost frontier model and the other from the distribution-free model. The results show that x-inefficiencies not only vary by country but by size and specialization. Firms in Finland and France have the lowest x-inefficiency, while firms in the United Kingdom have the highest. On average, small firms are more cost efficient than large firms worldwide. Firms grouped into those offering single or specialized services also operate more cost efficiently than those offering a combination of life and non-life services (combined firms). The results also indicate that the x-inefficiency estimates derived from the stochastic cost frontier model are more suitable for this sample of data than those derived from the distribution-free model.

Donni and Fecher (1997) measure the technical efficiency (TE) levels in 15 Organisation for Economic Co-operation and Development (OECD) insurance industries over the period 1983–1991 and decompose productivity changes into technical progress and efficiency variations. The study finds that growth in productivity observed in all countries is essentially due to improvements in technical progress. This is a comprehensive comparative study of efficiency of the OECD insurance markets. The study assumes significance since the time period is that of increasing integration and deregulation of the market.

A paper by Cummins and Zi (1998) applies frontier cost-efficiency methodologies to a data set consisting of 445 life insurers over the period 1988–1992. The different models attempted give significantly divergent estimates of efficiency for the in-sample insurers. The efficiency rankings are quite well-preserved among the econometric methodologies, but the rank correlations are found to be lower between the econometric and mathematical programming categories and between alternative mathematical programming methods. Thus, the choice of method has had a significant effect on the results. Most of the insurers in the sample display either increasing or decreasing returns to scale, and stock and mutual insurers are found to be equally efficient after controlling for firm size.

In the 1980s and the 1990s, the US life industry experienced an unprecedented wave of mergers and acquisitions (M&As). In this context, Cummins et al. (1999) examine the relationship between M&As, efficiency and scale economies in the US life insurance industry. They estimate cost and revenue efficiency over the period 1988–1995 using DEA. The Malmquist methodology is used to measure changes in efficiency over time. The results suggest that the acquired firms achieve greater efficiency gains than firms that have not been involved in mergers or acquisitions. Firms operating with non-decreasing returns to scale (NDRS) and financially vulnerable firms are more likely to be acquisition targets. Overall, M&As in the life insurance industry have had a beneficial effect on efficiency.

Greene and Segal (2004) explore the relationship between cost inefficiency and profitability in the US life insurance industry. They derive cost efficiency using the stochastic frontier (SF) method allowing the mean inefficiency to vary with organizational form and the outputs. The results suggest that cost inefficiency in the life insurance industry is substantial relative to earnings and that inefficiency is negatively associated with profitability measures such as the return on equity (RoE). The analysis of inefficiency and organizational form suggests that stock (shareholder-owned) companies are as efficient and profitable as mutual (policy holder-owned) companies.

A Translog cost function is estimated by Hao and Chou (2005) for 26 Taiwan life insurance companies over the period of 1977–1999. Here, they use the distribution-free approach (DFA) and Battese and Coelli (DFP) model to estimate inefficiency. The research suggests that (1) assets excluded from solvency regulations are potentially productive to the firm; (2) firms with a larger market share are more profitable; (3) diversification of product strategy is unable to help a firm improve its operational efficiency because Taiwan's life insurance firms always observe the standardized policy regulation; (4) if the firm is increasing its ordinary life insurance premium revenue, then the firm must be seeing an improvement in its investments; and (5) with price of claims rising, the firm sees a downside in the price of labour.

Cummins and Misas (2006) discuss the effects of deregulation and consolidation in financial services markets by analysing the Spanish insurance industry. The sample period 1989–1998 includes the introduction of the EU's Third Generation Insurance Directives, which deregulated the EU insurance market. Deregulation has led to dramatic changes in the Spanish insurance market; the number of firms declined by 35%, average firm size increased by 275% and unit prices declined significantly in both life and non-life insurance. They analyse the causes and effects of consolidation using modem frontier efficiency analysis to estimate cost, technical and allocative efficiency. Malmquist analysis is also used to measure total factor productivity (TFP) change. The results show that many small, inefficient and financially underperforming firms are eliminated from the market due to insolvency or liquidation. As a result, the market experiences significant growth in TFP over the sample period. Consolidation not only reduces the number of firms operating with increasing returns to scale but also increase the number operating with decreasing returns to scale. Hence, many large firms should focus on improving efficiency by adopting best practices rather than on further growth.

Wei Huang (2007) calculates the efficiency, especially the cost efficiency and profit efficiency of China's insurance industry for the period 1999–2004. The results show that for the cost efficiency, the life insurance industry, non-state-owned companies and foreign companies are superior to the property insurance industry. But for the profit efficiency, while the life insurance industry still surpasses the property insurance industry, the state-owned companies and domestic companies are better than their counterparts.

Cummins and Xie (2008) analyse the productivity and efficiency effects of M&As in the US P-L insurance industry during the period 1994–2003 using DEA and MPIs. They wanted to determine whether M&As are value-enhancing, value-neutral or value-reducing. The analysis examines efficiency and productivity change for acquirers, acquisition targets and non-M&A firms. They also examine the firm characteristics associated with becoming an acquirer or target through probit analysis. The results provide evidence that M&As in P-L insurance are value-enhancing. Acquiring firms achieve more revenue efficiency gains than non-acquiring firms, and target firms experience greater cost and allocative efficiency growth than non-targets. Factors other than efficiency enhancement are important factors in P-L insurer M&As. Financially vulnerable insurers are significantly more likely to become acquisition targets, consistent with corporate control theory. However, there is no evidence of scale economies playing an important role in the insurance M&A.

Eling and Luhnen (2008) provide an overview and some new evidence on frontier efficiency measurement in the insurance industry. Different methodologies, countries, organizational forms and company sizes are compared, considering life and non-life insurers. The study finds a steady technical and cost-efficiency growth in international insurance markets from 2002 to 2006, with large differences across countries. Denmark and Japan have the highest average efficiency, whereas the Philippines is the least efficient.

Qiu and Chen (2006) evaluate the relative efficiency of Chinese life insurers during 2000–2003, using DEA, estimate the technical efficiencies, pure technical efficiencies and scale efficiencies for different groups of life insurers. The results indicate that the TE scores of life insurers in China are dispersed. The traditional life insurers are technical efficient during the sample years. This reflects the market situation that traditional life insurers still have the monopoly power and smaller life insurers are not competitive enough. The result also shows that the average TE of the life insurance industry is decreasing year by year. On the one hand, the efficiency of newcoming insurer is forced to be low by large investment and delayed return. On the other hand, life insurers face more furious competition and greater challenge in China.

Lin et al. (2009) again adopt DEA to analyse the business efficiency of Taiwan's life insurance industry for the period 2005–2009. The research results show that the average TE of Taiwan's life insurance industry is relatively low and most life insurance companies need to enhance and improve efficiency. Most of the insurance companies continuously show increase in productivity. The average productivity of various life insurance companies has grown by 4.1% during 2008–2009.

Saad and Idris (2011) examine the efficiency of the life insurance industry in Brunei and Malaysia. DEA is used to explore the contributions of technical and efficiency change to the growth of productivity in the Malaysian and Brunei life insurance industries by applying the generalized output-oriented Malmquist index for the year 2000–2005. The output–input data consists of a panel of nine life insurance firms in Malaysia and two in Brunei. This study utilizes two inputs and two outputs, namely commission and management as well as premium and net investment income, respectively. It is found that, on average, the TFP of the life insurance industry is mainly due to both efficiency and technical changes where the main source of the efficiency change is scale efficiency (SE) rather than pure efficiency.

A paper by Khalid et al. (2012) estimates the TE of insurance companies (both life and non-life) in Gulf Cooperation Council (GCC) countries using DEA methodology and MPI to decompose the change in the efficiency into an intrinsic component reflecting the individual change in TE and a second component reflecting the impact of the change in the market technology on the individual technical efficiencies of insurance companies. The study considers 39 insurance firms in the region, with a panel data covering the period 2005–2007. The authors found that the insurance industry in the GCC is moderately efficient and there is large room for improvement.

2.2.2 *Some Indian Studies*

Research on efficiency of the Indian life insurance industry is very limited. Most of the past studies analyse the structure and financial performance of the insurance industry. However, few have employed DEA to evaluate efficiency/productivity of the life insurance companies in India. Tone and Sahoo (2005) for the first time study efficiency of the life insurance sector by employing a new variant of DEA model to examine the performance of LIC of India using time-series data. The findings show a significant heterogeneity in the cost efficiency scores over the period of 19 years. According to the authors, a decline in performance after 1994–1995 can be taken as evidence of increasing allocative inefficiencies arising from the huge initial fixed cost undertaken by LIC in modernizing its operations. A significant increase in cost efficiency in 2000–2001 however indicates that LIC may now be realizing a benefit from such modernization. Results from a sensitivity analysis are in broad agreement with the main findings of this study.

Sinha (2007) assesses the TFP growth in the life insurance industry for the period 2003–2005 using MPI. A comparison of TE scores of the life insurance companies indicates that the private insurance companies are still way behind LIC. Under the assumption of constant returns to scale (CRS), the inefficient firms are penalized more in terms of distance from the best-practice frontier. The mean TE score of the life insurers under CRS is much lower than that under variable returns to scale (VRS). For all the observed years, LIC and SBI Life have a TE score of 1. All other life insurance firms are technically inefficient (TE score of <1). In the years 2002–2003 and 2003–2004, excepting LIC all other insures exhibit increasing returns to scale. In 2004–2005, ING Vysya and Max New York Life exhibit decreasing returns to scale. All the life insurers exhibit positive TFP growth. Obviously, the TFP growth rate of the private life insurers is much higher than LIC. Among the private life insurers, Kotak Life has the highest TFP growth rate followed by Aviva Life insurance.

Sinha and Chatterjee (2009) calculate cost efficiency of the life insurance companies in India for the period 2002–2003 to 2006–2007 using the new cost-efficiency approach suggested by Tone (2002). The study follows the value-added approach and considers two output proxies, benefits paid to the customers and net premium mobilized, and two inputs, operating expenses and commission expenses. The results suggest an upward trend in cost efficiency of the observed life insurers during 2002–2003 and 2004–2005. However, the trend reverses for the next two years, that is, 2005–2006 and 2006–2007. This may be due to the fact that during the initial years of observation mean cost efficiency of the private life insurers was rising but the trend reversed in 2005–2006 and 2006–2007.

Sinha (2010) compares efficiency of 15 life insurance companies in India for 2005–2006 to 2008–2009 using the old and new revenue maximizing approaches. Both the approaches indicate LIC to be efficient for the observed years followed very closely by Sahara Life. However, the old approach heavily penalizes the technically inefficient firms. Dutta and Sengupta (2011) employ a panel data set of 14 life insurance companies for the period 2004–2009 to evaluate their efficiency scores by using DEA and calculating the SE. The results render light on policy design and implementations for future development of the life insurance industry in India.

Khan and Mitra (2012) use the window analysis developed by Klopp (1985) to compare the performance of the major life insurance companies operating in India using a two-output two-input framework. The window approach evaluates firms on the basis of a panel of observations and thus is different from the conventional DEA. In the conventional DEA, TE for any particular decision-making unit (DMU) is measured by evaluating the DMU in light of all the DMUs under observation for the time period. The study encompasses 18 life insurance companies for the period 2007–2008 to 2012–2013. The results suggest that there still exists a huge gap between LIC of India and other life insurance companies in terms of TE. However, they suggest that the gap is expected to come down in future as the industry matures with increase in insurance penetration and density levels in India.

Chakraborty and Sengupta (2012) attempt a comparison of performance and efficiency in terms of catch-up efficiency scores, frontier-shift efficiency scores and Malmquist TFP growth index for a 7-year period ranging from 2003–2004 to 2009–2010. LICI exhibited a relative catch-up efficiency of 1 and the private life insurers such as Kotak and ING Vysya score of more than 1 over the period. Further, a comparison of the relative frontier-shift efficiency scores of the life insurers for the 7-year period from 2003–2004 to 2009–2010 reflects that the public-sector life insurer is marginally ahead of its private sector counterparts with respect to efficiency in frontier technology over the years. Moreover, LICI exhibited a consistent relative TFP change index score of more than 1 over the 7-year time period, thereby indicating a relative progress in TFP growth.

Noronh and Shinde (2012) evaluate the cost efficiency of all the life insurance companies for the period 2000–2001 to 2009–2010. The study involves calculation of cost efficiency score of life insurance sector in India with the DEA. LIC has consistently secured a cost-efficiency score of 1 in all the years from 2000–2001 to 2009–2010 and scored the highest rank for all the years under study. Thus, LIC has consistently been a cost-efficient organization. While in the case of the private life insurance companies, the cost-efficiency score has been inconsistent.

Chakraborty et al. (2012) investigated TE and productivity growth in the Indian life insurance industry in the era of deregulation. The study uses DEA and MPI to measure and decompose TE and productivity growth, respectively. The results suggest that the growth in overall productivity is mainly attributed to improvement in efficiency. Higher pure technical efficiency (PTE) and lower-scale efficiency indicate that the insurance firms have generally moved away from the optimal scale over the study period. The truncated regression exploring the main drivers of efficiency in the long run finds that the claims ratio, distribution ratio and firm size influence TE positively. The study also finds that firms having both life and non-life businesses are more efficient than firms doing life insurance business alone.

Nandi (2014) measures the relative performance efficiency of 13 life insurance companies of India (1 public sector and 12 private sector) covering a period of 10 years from 2002–2003 to 2011–2012. The study uses DEA technique to measure efficiency individually, year wise, sector wise and as a whole. The study employs two inputs and two outputs, namely commission paid and operating expenses as well as premium and net benefit, respectively. Since this study attempts to maximize output, so output-oriented DEA is being used. The results of the study shows that overall life insurers carrying life insurance business at an average TE of 82.6%, PTE of 87.5% and SE of 94.7%. On the other hand, in individual and sector-wise performance analysis, LIC performs better as compared to others.

The review of both international and Indian studies reveals that efficiency in developed countries is on an average higher than that in emerging markets and that technical progress has increased productivity and efficiency around the world. However, in Indian context, there are a limited number of empirical studies available on the life insurance industry, measuring productivity and efficiency of individual life insurers and the overall industry. All the past studies on the Indian life insurance industry, measuring efficiency and productivity, are either based on a single insurance company with time-series data period or a panel of insurance companies with a smaller sample period. The present study improves upon the past ones by considering the longest available period, with a larger sample of insurers. The efficiency and the productivity are examined for this period, employing DEA.

2.3 Data and Methodology

2.3.1 *Data Description*

The sample consists of 13 life insurance companies listed in the Appendix, having operations consistently in all the years of the sample period 2002–2003 to 2014–2015 (13 years). The source of the data used is collected from the IRDAI's (regulator) *Handbook of Indian Insurance Statistics and Public Disclosers of Insurance Companies*, and 2014–2015 is the latest year for which data is available at present. All the life insurance indicators are expressed in real terms by deflating by wholesale price index (WPI) with base year 2004–2005.

2.3.2 *Inputs and Outputs*

An important step in efficiency analysis is the selection of input and output. Indeed, the result can be misleading or meaningless if these are not properly defined. This problem is especially acute in the service sector such as insurance, banking, etc., where many outputs are intangible and many prices are implicit, resulting in measurement difficulties. The best way to resolve this is to identify the services provided by such firms and find measurable proxies that are highly correlated with those services. There has been considerable disagreement in the literature over the appropriate proxies to be used as the output for the insurance services. Different sets of variables are considered in the existing literature to analyse efficiency of insurance firms.

2.3.2.1 Inputs

The widely accepted inputs in insurance in the literature may be classified into three main categories: (1) labour, (ii) business service and materials, and (3) capital.

- *Labour* is the most important input in the financial service industry. In insurance companies, no raw material is required and cost of labour is the major component of cost. It is defined as the number of employees and agents in the insurance company. In this study, '*individual agents* (IA)' is used as labour input as company-wise number of employees is not available.

- *Business service and materials* consist of all operating expenses other than labour and capital expenses. Most of these expenses are related directly to selling and servicing policies. The *total commission* (TC) is used as the input for business services and materials in this study.
- *Capital* comprises of two components: *financial capital*, defined as book value of equity plus the asset valuation reserve (AVR); and *physical capital*, defined as the sum of capital expenses – rent, rental of equipment and depreciation. Many studies (Khalid et al. 2012; Cummins and Misas 2006) have included equity capital as an input. The rationale for the use of equity capital is that insurers must maintain equity capital to back the promise to settle claims even if losses are higher than expected and also to satisfy regulatory requirements. The rationale for the use of *debt capital* (*DC*) is similar to that for the use of deposits as an input in banking, that is, insurers raise debt capital by issuing insurance and annuity policies and invest the capital as part of the intermediation function. However, debt capital is not always used as an input in banking or insurance studies because reserves for insurers and deposits for banks have some characteristics of both inputs and outputs. In addition, to the extent that the definition of insurance output and output price accounts for the time value of money, it is probably not necessary to include debt capital as an input. In this study, we employ two inputs, *equity share capital as equity capital* (EC) and *total liabilities as debt capital* (DC).

2.3.2.2 Outputs

In efficiency literature, there are mainly three principal approaches to measure outputs in the insurance industry: (1) the asset or intermediation approach, (2) the user-cost approach and (3) the value-added approach. The value-added approach assumes that the insurer provides three main services for which volume output proxies must be defined: through the *first* service, risk-pooling and risk-bearing. Insurers create value added by operating a risk pool, collecting premiums from policyholders and redistributing most of them to customers who have incurred losses. They also reduce their customers' risks by holding capital to absorb unexpected losses. The *second* service, 'real' financial services relating to insured losses, means that insurers create value added for their policyholders by providing real services such as financial planning (life) or the design of coverage

Table 2.1 Choice of input and output variables

Inputs	*Outputs*
(a) IA: number of individual agents	(a) NBPC: benefits paid to customers (net)
(b) TC: total commission	(b) LAL: liquid assets to liabilities
(c) EC: equity share capital	
(d) DC: total liabilities	

programmes (P-L). The *third* service is intermediation, where insurers add value by acting as financial intermediaries that invest assets, which policyholders provide by way of their premiums (Cummins et al. 1999). Considering the nature of insurance industry, value-added approach appears to be the most appropriate to analyse efficiency and productivity of the life insurance firms in India.

To proxy the risk-pooling/risk-bearing function, either premiums or incurred benefits (life) and present value of losses (P-L) have been used. However, there is an intense debate as to suitability of premiums as proxy because they represent price-times quantity of output and not output (Yuengert 1993). This suggests a loss-based measure, which has been used in the majority of existing insurance efficiency studies. This could be losses incurred or life insurance incurred benefits plus addition to reserves (Yuengert 1993). Benefit paid is an appropriate measure because the purpose of insurance is to pool the experience of all policyholders and pay claims to those who suffer loss during a given period.

Table 2.1 gives an overview of the inputs and outputs used in this study, and Table 2.2 presents the descriptive statistics of the variables employed.

2.3.3 Methodology

This study employs DEA and MPI to assess the efficiency and change in productivity of life insurance companies in India for the period 2002–2003 to 2014–2015. The DEA is employed mainly due to two reasons. First, it enables decomposing cost efficiency into its components – technical and allocative efficiency as well as decomposing technical to PTE and SE. Secondly, the DEA-based Malmquist approach measures the evolution of productivity and efficiency over time. Thus, the use of DEA permits us to use the same methodology consistently throughout the chapter. To estimate the results, the study employs *DEA-Solver Software Pro-8.0 version* to measure

Table 2.2 Descriptive statistics of inputs and outputs (I/O)

I/O (Rs. in crores)	*Min*	*Max*	*Mean*	*SD*	*Min*	*Max*	*Mean*	*SD*
		2002–2003				**2003–2004**		
Benefits paid	0.1	20,530.4	1,580.4	5,693.8	0.5	23,923.8	1,845.7	6,633.6
Liquid assets to liabilities	5.6	21.9	13.2	4.9	4.6	26.3	11.6	5.7
Agents	1,454	988,358	82,188	272,335	2,181	1,098,910	97,322	301,190
Total commissions	1.7	4,998.6	396.4	1,382.8	5.5	5,733.8	473.7	1,580.7
Equity capital	5.0	425.0	171.8	96.5	5.0	675.0	237.4	155.8
Debt capital	96.5	277,160.3	21,620.7	76,780.4	181.7	346,022.5	27,259.5	95,777.8
		2006–2007				**2007–2008**		
Benefits paid	20.8	53,286.5	4,285.5	14,724.8	34.7	56,550.3	4,744.3	15,574.7
Liquid assets to liabilities	4.2	11.8	7.7	2.0	2.8	11.5	6.6	2.5
Agents	18,019	1,103,047	150,424.4615	295,307.5135	22,360	1,193,744	187,780.5385	315,128.645
Total commissions	80.2	9,169.1	940.4	2,483.7	105.5	9,568.1	1,123.2	2,563.8
Equity capital	5.0	1,312.3	591.7	323.2	5.0	1,401.1	860.6	426.2
Debt capital	1,222.7	625,957.0	52,177.9	172,451.2	2,718.1	776,904.9	67,366.9	213,328.9
		2010–2011				2011–2012		
Benefits paid	477.9	111,241.2	10,904.3	30,270.1	758.9	117,472.1	11,673.3	31,866.0
Liquid assets to liabilities	0.9	4.8	2.9	1.1	1.3	7.2	3.7	1.7
Agents	232.7	1,337,064	189,613.6154	351,037.0333	19,126	1,278,234	168,677.9231	337,869.4806
Total commissions	87.3	13,308.7	1,366.5	3,594.3	93.6	14,035.6	1,388.0	3,805.3
Equity capital	5.0	2,004.9	1,343.0	727.2	100.0	2,004.9	1,360.0	718.8
Debt capital	7,033.5	1,282,128.6	120,339.3	349,525.5	7,463.3	1,380,116.6	129,622.5	376,484.6
		2013–2014				**2014–2015**		
Benefits paid	1,507.1	78,230.5	13,321.0	22,352.8	1,038.4	93,009.9	10,474.3	24,909.4
Liquid assets to liabilities	1.5	6.9	4.1	1.7	0.0	12.5	4.6	2.9

(*continued*)

Table 2.2 (continued)

I/O (Rs. in crores)	*Min*	*Max*	*Mean*	*SD*	*Min*	*Max*	*Mean*	*SD*
Agents	17,017	1,163,604	151,525.6154	306,391.4629	17,017	1,163,604	152,717.5385	306,057.8401
Total commissions	77.8	407,546.4	31,637.3	112,946.8	77.8	10,012.3	1,081.9	2,694.2
Equity capital	100.0	2,012.9	1,378.9	723.6	0.0	2,012.9	1,231.3	796.4
Debt capital	9,890.0	1,992,078.5	186,673.6	543,172.2	10,523.4	2,123,972.2	201,087.8	578,467.6
			2004–2005				**2005–2006**	
Benefits paid	2.6	28,440.5	2,211.6	7,880.8	6.0	33,927.1	2,708.4	9,381.6
Liquid assets to liabilities	4.8	35.4	11.1	7.8	3.7	13.7	8.8	3.1
Agents	2,080	1,041,737	93,283	285,408	5,046	1,052,283	108,800	285,012
Total commissions	7.9	6,245.2	546.0	1,713.2	14.3	7,094.9	663.7	1,934.6
Equity capital	5.0	925.0	322.7	213.4	5.0	1,185.0	431.5	284.2
Debt capital	314.2	416,910.4	33,432.1	115,227.5	521.4	531,390.4	43,034.9	146,751.8
			2008–2009				**2009–2010**	
Benefits paid	76.7	52,478.1	4,488.0	14,430.3	172.5	79,130.7	7,342.4	21,651.0
Liquid assets to liabilities	2.0	8.3	5.3	2.0	1.0	5.6	3.3	1.2
Agents	30,838	1,344,856	214,433.8462	348,081.7419	23,753	1,402,807	213,083.1538	364,414.7105
Total commissions	110.4	10,033.2	1,171.1	2,674.5	120.8	12,110.3	1,342.5	3,244.3
Equity capital	5.0	1,879.5	1,178.8	620.0	5.0	1,969.5	1,279.9	704.9
Debt capital	3,696.9	841,272.9	74,691.4	230,497.5	5,807.1	1,117,416.2	103,507.7	305,009.8
			2012–2013				**2012–2013**	
Benefits paid	1,193.4	134,881.3	14,584.2	36,325.5	1,153.1	158,015.5	16,393.2	42,681.1
Liquid assets to liabilities	1.8	9.4	4.5	2.1	1.4	9.2	4.5	2.1
Agents	17,470	1,172,983	156,894.5385	309,054.318	13,448	1,195,916	160,834.7692	315,353.8808
Total commissions	103.5	14,768.0	1,443.9	4,010.0	78.5	16,681.3	1,564.1	4,547.4
Equity capital	100.0	2,012.9	1,364.0	722.0	1,00.0	2,012.9	1,369.1	720.1
Debt capital	7,925.1	2,402,581.0	325,227.7	748,886.5	8,794.3	1,724,457.6	160,299.4	470,476.7

Benefits paid: in Rs. crores; liquid assets to liabilities ratio in %; agents: in number; total commissions: in Rs. crores; equity capital: in Rs. crores; debt capital: in Rs. crores the TE, SE, PTE and Malmquist productivity growth index as well the catch up and frontier shift of the 13 life insurers for the study period.

The research design calls for the assessment of the relative TE of each firm considered in the sample and the identification of the main sources of inefficiency. The TE can be further decomposed into two efficiency indices to determine the sources of overall technical inefficiency. The first one is PTE index, which determines the insurers' efficiency relative to a frontier that exhibits constant as well as VRS. The other index, the SE index, measures whether or not the insurance companies operate at CRS or at increasing or decreasing returns to scale.

In practice, the TE scores are obtained by running the original DEA model under the CRS assumption, known as the Charnes, Cooper and Rhodes (CCR) model (Charnes et al. 1978). The PTE scores are obtained by running the DEA model under assumption of VRS, known as Banker, Charnes and Cooper (BCC) model (Banker et al. 1984; Banker et al. 1996). Any significant difference between the TE and PTE scores indicates the existence of scale inefficiency, a deviation from operating at the appropriate scale. The SE scores can be computed by means of the ratio of the overall TE to that of PTE, as explained in Coelli et al. (2005):

$$\text{Technical efficiency} = \text{Pure technical efficiency} \times \text{Scale efficiency}$$
$$\text{TE} = \text{PTE} \times \text{SE}$$

2.3.3.1 Measuring Efficiency

Farrell (1957) suggested constructing the efficiency frontier using the observed sample of firms in the industry. The firms in the constructed frontier are defined to be efficient. Each firm is compared to a point on the efficient unit iso-surface and then a relative measure of efficiency is determined. So, measuring efficiency and identifying peers by graphical techniques is only possible in simple cases. However, when a firm has many inputs and outputs, more sophisticated techniques need to be used to solve this problem. There are two main approaches (parametric and non-parametric) in efficient frontier analysis, which represent the empirical foundation to Farrell's best-practice concept (Farrell 1957) for the estimation of efficiency. The main advantage of econometric/parametric approaches [stochastic frontier approach (SFA), DFA and thick frontier approach (TFA)] is that it allows firms to be off the frontier due to random error as well as inefficiency and, consequently, do not count purely random error as inefficiency. But it requires specification of functional form such as Translog to estimate the frontier and distributional assumptions in order to recover the efficiency estimates.

However, the non-parametric approach (DEA, Free Disposal Hull (FDH)) avoids the specification error because it is not necessary to specify either functional form or distributional assumptions. In most applications of methodology, any departure from the frontier is measured as inefficiency, that is, random error or bad luck is not separated out. The DEA computes the 'best practice' efficient frontiers based on convex combination of firms in the industry. The method enables one to estimate production, cost and revenue frontiers and to decompose efficiency into different components like cost efficiency, profit efficiency and TE.

Data Envelopment Analysis

The idea of the non-parametric efficiency approach originated in Farrell (1957), but the empirical work had been limited to a single-output case and did not deal with applications where large data sets with multiple input–outputs were involved. Moreover, this mathematical programming idea did not receive much detailed attention for about two decades, until the paper by Charnes et al. (1978) was published. In this classic paper, the authors proposed a mathematical programming method, termed DEA, for assessing the performance of a set of homogeneous entities called DMUs, which convert multiple inputs into multiple outputs. This approach forms an empirical production frontier or envelopment surface and measures and calculates efficiency relative to the constructed frontier. Since the pioneering work by Charnes et al. (1978), numerous papers have appeared, which have extended and applied the DEA methodology. Seiford (1997) lists over 400 papers in a comprehensive bibliography, and Cooper et al. (2007) list over 2000 DEA references. Such rapid growth and widespread acceptance of DEA is testimony to its strengths and applicability. In the literature, DEA is typically represented as a generalized ratio:

$$\text{Efficiency ratio} = \frac{\text{Weighted sum of outputs}}{\text{Weighted sum of inputs}} = \frac{\sum_i Q_i Y_i}{\sum_j P_j X_j}$$

where Y_i and X_j are outputs and inputs respectively while Q_i and P_j are firm-specific weights to be calculated by the DEA technique. Each company is given a single efficiency score from 0 to 1. The closer the score to 1, the firm is more efficient. DEA allocates specific weights (Q_i and P_j) for each company on the basis of giving the highest possible score. This is sometimes expressed as putting a company 'in the best possible light'. The basic DEA models and the backbone of efficiency studies in the literature are briefly discussed next.

(i) *CCR Model*

The CCR model is the most basic DEA model, which was proposed by Charnes et al. (1978). This model is used to measure the overall TE of DMUs. They introduced a measure of efficiency for each DMU that was obtained as a maximum of a ratio of weighted outputs to weighted inputs. The ratio for every DMU has to be ≤1. Here, it is possible to reduce the multiple-output/multiple-input situation for each DMU to a single virtual output and a single virtual input ratio. This ratio provides a measure of efficiency for a given DMU, which is a function of the weights of the virtual input–output combination. Formally, the efficiency for each DMU can be obtained by the following mathematical programming approach:

$$\left.\begin{aligned} &\text{Max } h_0 = \frac{\Sigma_{r=1}^{s} u_r y_{r0}}{\Sigma_{i=1}^{m} v_i x_{i0}} \\ &\text{subject to} \\ &\frac{\Sigma_{r=1}^{s} u_r y_{rj}}{\Sigma_{i=1}^{m} v_i x_{ij}} \leq 1; j = 1, 2, 3, \ldots, n \\ &u_r, v_i \geq 0; \quad r = 1, 2, \ldots, s; \; I = 1, 2, 3, \ldots, m \end{aligned}\right\} \tag{2.1}$$

where x_{ij} is the observed amount of input of the ith type of the jth DMU ($x_{ij} > 0$, $i = 1, 2, \ldots, m$, $j = 1, 2, \ldots, n$) and y_{rj} is the observed amount of output of the rth type for the jth DMU ($y_{rj} > 0$, $r = 1, 2, \ldots, s$, $j = 1, 2, \ldots, n$). In other words, jth DMU uses an m-dimensional input vector to produce an s-dimensional output vector. Here, (x_{i0}, y_{r0}) is the input–output vector of the producer being evaluated. The objective function h_0 tries to maximize the ratio of virtual output to virtual input subject to the constraint that this kind of ratio for each DMU must be ≤1.

The variables u_r and v_i are the weights of output and input, which must be non-negative and are determined by the aforementioned programming approach. However, a notable problem with this particular fractional formulation is that it has an infinite number of solutions; if (u^*, v^*) is optimal, then $(\alpha u^*, \alpha v^*)$ will also be optimal for non-negative α. Thus, Charnes et al. (1978) have transformed this problem into an equivalent linear programming problem. They added an additional constraint $\sum_{i=1}^{m} v_i x_{i0} = 1$ so that this transformation is achieved and the non-uniqueness problem identified earlier can be avoided. The notation changes from (u, v) to (μ, v) to reflect the transformation. The new linear programming problem is equivalent to the equations in Eq. 2.1. It can be written as

$$\left.\begin{array}{l} \max_{\mu} z_0 = \sum_{r=1}^{s} u_r y_{r0} \\ \sum_{r=1}^{s} u_r y_{rj} - \sum_{i=1}^{m} v_i x_{ij} \leq 0, j = 1, 2, \ldots, n \\ \sum_{i=1}^{m} v_i x_{i0} = 1 \\ \mu_r, v_i \geq 0; r = 1, 2, \ldots, m \end{array}\right\} \quad (2.2)$$

These equations are known as the multiplier form of the DEA linear programming problem. The dual for DMU_0 can be derived as

$$\left.\begin{array}{ll} \min_{\lambda} z_0 = \theta_0{}^{\text{CCR}} & \\ \text{subject to} & \\ \sum_{j=1}^{n} \lambda_j y_{rj} \geq y_{r0}, & r = 1, 2, \ldots, s \\ \sum_{j=1}^{n} \lambda_j x_{ij} \leq \theta_0{}^{\text{CCR}} x_{i0}, & i = 1, 2, \ldots, m \\ \lambda_j \geq 0, & j = 1, 2, \ldots, n \end{array}\right\} \quad (2.3)$$

The aforementioned problem is referred to as the envelopment form of DEA. Optimal solutions (θ, λ) are obtained for each of the DMUs being evaluated. The value of θ is the efficiency score for the particular DMU_0 and this efficiency score is a radial measure of TE, according to the Debreu (1951) and Farrell (1957) definition. A set of constraints assures that the value of θ is always less than or equal to unity and the efficiency score for each observed DMU is relative to other DMUs. DMUs for which $\theta = 1$ are identified as the technically efficient while when $\theta < 1$ we have a relatively inefficient DMU. The optimal λ can identify a project (boundary) point located on the constructed production frontier when the problem seeks the radial contraction of the input vector. Färe et al. (1994) point out that the CCR model imposes a feasible production set which is closed and convex, and presents constant returns-to-scale and strong disposability of inputs and outputs.

(ii) *BCC Model*

In Charnes et al.'s (1978) original paper, it was pointed out that the model assumes CRS. This assumption is appropriate only when all DMUs are operating at an optimal scale. But in the real world many factors such as constraints on finance, government regulations and imperfect competition may cause some DMUs not to operate at the optimal scale. Therefore, in this situation, the measures of TE using the CCR model will be confounded by scale inefficiencies. Subsequently, Banker et al. (1984) drop the CRS assumption. They propose a model that takes into account the effect of returns to scale within DMUs called the VRS model or *BCC model*. The purpose of the VRS assumption is to attempt to determine the most efficient scale size for each DMU and at the same time to identify its TE. Thus, the primary difference between BCC model and the CCR model is the treatment of returns to scale. The CCR model is the treatment evaluation of CRS. The BCC version is more flexible and allows VRS.

Banker et al. (1984) add a convexity condition for $\lambda_j : \sum_{j=1}^{n} \lambda_j = 1$, which ensures that an inefficient DMU is only compared with similar sized DMUs. With this added constraint, the reference set is changed from the conical hull in the case of the CCR model to the convex hull in the case of the VRS model. This change ensures that the tested DMU is compared with a lesser number of combinations. Thus, TE scores provided by the CCR model are greater than or equal to those in the BBC model.

The input-oriented BCC model for DMU_0 in envelopment form can be written formally as

$$\left.\begin{array}{lll}\min & \theta_0{}^{\mathrm{BCC}} - \varepsilon\left(\sum_{\mathrm{i}=1}^{\mathrm{m}} \mathrm{s}_{\mathrm{i}}^{-} + \sum_{\mathrm{i}=1}^{\mathrm{s}} \mathrm{s}_{\mathrm{r}}^{+}\right) & \\ & \theta,\lambda, s_i^{-}, s_i^{+} & \\ \multicolumn{3}{l}{\text{subject to}} \\ \multicolumn{2}{l}{\sum_{j=1}^{n} \lambda_j y_{rj} - s_r^{+} = y_{r0};} & r = 1, 2, \ldots, s \\ \multicolumn{2}{l}{\sum_{j=1}^{n} \lambda_j x_{ij} + s_i^{-} = \theta_0 x_{i0};} & i = 1, 2, \ldots, m \\ \multicolumn{2}{l}{\sum_{j=1}^{n} \lambda_j = 1} & \\ \multicolumn{2}{l}{\lambda_j, s_r^{+}, s_i^{-} \geq 0,} & j = 1, 2, \ldots, n\end{array}\right\} \quad (2.4)$$

Solving the aforementioned problem for each DMU, BCC efficiency scores, θ, are obtained. These scores are also called the *pure technical score* since they are obtained from a model which allows for VRS and eliminates the problem of SE from the analysis. Furthermore, if $\sum_{j=1}^{n} \lambda_j = 1$ is replaced by $0 \leq \sum_{j=1}^{n} \lambda_j \leq 1$, then the non-increasing returns to scale (NIRS) envelopment model is obtained. That is, if we replace $\sum_{j=1}^{n} \lambda_j = 1$ with $\sum_{j=1}^{n} \lambda_j \geq 1$, then we obtain the NDRS envelopment model.

In the preceding analysis, DEA models are called *input-orientated* DEA models. *The input-orientated DEA model maximizes the proportional reduction in inputs as much as possible, given the current level of outputs.* On the other hand, it is also possible to seek the proportional augmentation in outputs keeping at most the current level of inputs. Thus, the output direction can also be applied in the aforementioned models. In the output-oriented models, the envelopment surface (efficiency frontier) in the model remains the same for both the VRS or CRS methods but the measures of inefficient firms may differ between the two methods. The choice of an appropriate orientation is made according to which quantities (inputs or outputs) the managers have most control over. Thus, for example, if producers are required to meet market demands, and if they can freely adjust input usage, then an input-oriented model seems to be appropriate. Or the firms may be given a fixed quantity of resources and asked to produce as much output as possible. Then an output-oriented model would be more appropriate. However, some researchers have pointed out that the choice of orientation has only a minor effect on the scores obtained and therefore it may not be a crucial issue.

2.3.3.2 Productivity Change

TFP growth is measured as the change in total outputs net of the change in total input usage. A good number of studies have explored the issue of TFP growth in the insurance industry in the global context. It is also important to measure the effects of changes in management practices and the introduction of new technologies. The MPI introduced by Caves et al. (1982) shows that productivity movements can be measured by a multi-input, multi-output Malmquist index when input and output data are available in physical units, so that no price index problems arise. They argue that the distance function $d(x, y)$ can be used in the construction of the Malmquist index and measure the Malmquist index of change between t and $t + 1$ as the ratio $[d^T\ (x^{t+1}, y^{t+1}) / d^T(x^t, y^t)]$. The Malmquist index of TFP change is derived as the geometric mean of two indices based on the technology for year t and year $t + 1$, respectively. In other words,

$$[M\left(x^{t+1}, y^{t+1}, x^t, y^t\right) = \left[\frac{d^t\left(x^{t+1}, y^{t+1}\right)}{d^t\left(x^t, y^t\right)} \times \frac{d^{t+1}\left(x^{t+1}, y^{t+1}\right)}{d^{t+1} + \left(x^t, y^t\right)}\right]^{1/2}$$

Equivalently,

$$M\left(x^{t+1}, y^{t+1}, x^t, y^t\right) = \frac{d^t\left(x^{t+1}, y^{t+1}\right)}{d^t\left(x^t, y^t\right)} \left[\frac{d^t\left(x^{t+1}, y^{t+1}\right)}{d^{t+1}\left(x^{t+1}, y^t + 1\right)} \times \frac{d^t\left(x^t, y^t\right)}{d^{t+1} + \left(x^t, y^t\right)}\right]^{1/2}$$

The ratio outside the brackets is the index of change in TE (i.e. catch-up index) between years t and $t + 1$, while the bracketed term is the index of change in technology (frontier-shift index) between two periods evaluated at x^t and x^{t+1}. Thus, MPI is decomposed into two components, namely a *catch-up index* and a *frontier-shift index.* The catch-up (recovery) term relates to the degree to which a DMU improves or worsens its efficiency, while the frontier-shift (or innovation) term reflects the change in efficiency frontiers between the two time periods and hence measures the change in the technology in the sector formed by the DMUs considered in the sample. In the present study, it is the life insurance industry in India.

$$\text{MPI} = (\text{catch up}) \times (\text{frontier shift})$$

The interpretation of the indices obtained from the decomposition of the MPI is

- Catch up > 1 indicates progress in relative efficiency from period t to $t + 1$. While (catch up) = 1 and (catch up) <1 indicate no change and regress in efficiency, respectively.
- Frontier shift > 1 indicates progress in the frontier technology around the corresponding DMU from the period t to $t + 1$. While (frontier shift) =1 and (frontier shift) <1 indicate the status quo and regress in the frontier technology, respectively.
- MPI > 1 implies that there has been progress in TFP, while MPI values of less than 1 (MPI < 1) and equal to 1 (MPI = 1) indicate deterioration in TFP and no productivity change, respectively.

2.4 Results and Discussion

2.4.1 TE and Its Decomposition

The DEA results in this study are based on the output maximization model, known as output-oriented approach. In this approach, the maximum output is determined while holding inputs constant. The DEA model was run twice, once under the CRS assumption and then under the VRS assumption. CRS assumes that there is no significant relationship between the scale of operations and efficiency, thus small insurance firms can be as efficient as large insurers in converting the specified inputs into the specified outputs. DEA under VRS assumption is run to check for scale inefficiency. The scale inefficiency may be understood as disproportional change in output compared with any change in inputs. The CRS efficiency score of each insurers measures its TE, which indicates the inefficiencies due to the input/output (I/O) configuration and the size of operations. On the other hand, VRS efficiency score represents PTE that is the measure of efficiency after eliminating the scale inefficiency. Therefore, SE score is calculated by dividing the TE score by the PTE score (SE = TE/PTE).

The efficiency (TE, PTE and SE) scores in our sample of 13 insurance firms is calculated for the period 2002–2003 to 2014–2015 and is reported in Table 2.4. A summary of the scores is also presented in Table 2.3. Table 2.3 and Fig. 2.1 indicate the average efficiency scores per year as well as for the whole study period for the sample of firms studied.

The average TE of all 13 life insurance companies in India for FY03 is 69.82% with a minimum score of 25.40% efficiency. However, in FY04 the average declined to 67.63%, with a minimum score of 7.90% with a standard deviation (SD) of 31.77%. However, in FY05, the average TE was back to 73.63% with a minimum efficiency score of 33.47% and an SD 27.31%. After FY05, the average TE scores trended upwards and reached the highest level of 94.12% in FY14, with an SD of 10.36% and a minimum score of 70.60%, which is the highest in the period of study. In FY15, the efficiency declined to 77.99% as PTE significantly declined.

The results indicate that LIC has consistently scored 1 throughout the study period, followed by Bajaj Allianz in 10 instances, while all other insurance companies scored 1 in patches. Among the private insurers, out of the top three companies in terms of market share, only SBI life has scored 1 since FY10, whereas the other two (HDFC Life and ICICI Prudential Life) have scored below 1 throughout the study period.

Table 2.3 Summary statistics of annual averages of technical efficiency scores

Year	*Efficiency measure*	*Mean (%)*	*SD (%)*	*Minimum (%)*	*Maximum (%)*	*No. of fully efficient firms*
FY15	**TE**	**77.99**	**31.18**	**18.86**	**100**	**8**
	PTE	81.56	26.15	30.58	100	8
	SE	91.88	13.13	61.65	100	8
FY14	**TE**	**94.12**	**10.36**	**70.60**	**100**	**9**
	PTE	94.69	9.58	72.60	100	9
	SE	99.31	1.42	95.39	100	9
FY13	**TE**	**90.55**	**16.50**	**50.45**	**100**	**8**
	PTE	92.46	14.29	59.33	100	9
	SE	97.43	4.34	85.02	100	8
FY12	**TE**	**91.38**	**13.88**	**59.06**	**100**	**8**
	PTE	95.81	8.61	76.26	100	9
	SE	94.95	8.37	75.54	100	8
FY11	**TE**	**89.14**	**16.76**	**48.47**	**100**	**8**
	PTE	94.01	11.10	67.18	100	9
	SE	94.09	9.56	72.15	100	8
FY10	**TE**	**85.07**	**20.19**	**50.14**	**100**	**8**
	PTE	90.04	14.51	63.65	100	8
	SE	93.58	10.67	66.31	100	8
FY09	**TE**	**85.93**	**17.10**	**55.28**	**100**	**5**
	PTE	92.13	10.13	77.40	100	7
	SE	92.49	10.49	70.70	100	5
FY08	**TE**	**86.80**	**15.25**	**55.53**	**100**	**6**
	PTE	92.62	11.23	64.17	100	8
	SE	93.33	8.59	77.01	100	6
FY07	**TE**	**84.67**	**24.43**	**33.15**	**100**	7
	PTE	90.40	18.15	48.72	100	8
	SE	92.41	15.22	55.20	100	7
FY06	**TE**	**75.89**	**25.47**	**26.98**	**100**	**5**
	PTE	83.98	24.06	29.55	100	7
	SE	90.48	13.58	55.62	100	5
FY05	**TE**	**73.63**	**27.31**	**33.47**	**100**	**4**
	PTE	80.22	28.99	33.86	100	8
	SE	92.68	10.42	64.13	100	4
FY04	**TE**	**67.63**	**31.77**	**7.90**	**100**	**4**
	PTE	73.91	31.91	17.38	100	6
	SE	88.54	15.38	45.43	100	4
FY03	**TE**	**69.82**	**32.90**	**8.24**	**100**	**6**
	PTE	76.80	26.51	25.40	100	6
	SE	85.51	20.40	32.43	100	6
Average (FY03–15)	**TE**	**81.84**	**22.22**	**38.97**	**100**	7
	PTE	**87.18**	**18.41**	**50.56**	**100**	**8**
	SE	**92.44**	**11.43**	**64.30**	**100**	7

Note: *TE*: Technical Efficiency, *PTE*: Pure Technical Efficiency and *SE*: Scale Efficiency

Table 2.4 Technical efficiency scores (TE, PTE and SE) of sample Indian life insurers

Insurer	*FY12*			*FY13*			*FY14*			*FY15*		
	TE	*PTE*	*SE*	*TE*	*PTE*	*SE*	*TE*	*PTE*	*SE*	*TE*	*PTE*	*SE*
Aviva	1	1	1	1	1	1	1	1	1	1	1	1
Bajaj Allianz	1	1	1	1	1	1	1	1	1	1	1	1
Birla Sun Life	0.7964	0.9991	0.7972	0.5045	0.5933	0.8502	0.7060	0.7260	0.9724	0.3200	0.4381	0.7304
HDFC Standard	0.5906	0.7818	0.7554	0.6430	0.6767	0.9502	0.7691	0.7737	0.9941	0.3655	0.4755	0.7687
ICICI Prudential	1	1	1	1	1	1	1	1	1	0.1886	0.3058	0.6165
Exide Life	1	1	1	1	1	1	1	1	1	1	1	1
Kotak Mahindra	1	1	1	1	1	1	1	1	1	1	1	1
Max Life	0.9322	1	0.9322	0.9307	0.9693	0.9602	0.8293	0.8695	0.9539	0.5972	0.6900	0.8655
PNB MetLife	1	1	1	0.7515	0.7802	0.9632	1	1	1	1.0000	1.0000	1.0000
Reliance	0.8737	0.9117	0.9584	1	1	1	1.0000	1.0000	1.0000	1	1	1
SBI Life	1	1	1	1	1	1	1	1	1	1	1	1
TATA AIA	0.6866	0.7626	0.9004	0.9415	1	0.9415	0.9312	0.9410	0.9897	0.6672	0.693	0.9627
LIC	1	1	1	1	1	1	1	1	1	1	1	1
Memo												
Average	0.91381	0.95809	0.9495	0.90547	0.92458	0.97425	0.9412	0.9469	0.9931	0.7799	0.8156	0.9188
SD	0.13883	0.08609	0.08371	0.16503	0.14295	0.04345	0.1036	0.0958	0.0142	0.3118	0.2615	0.1313
Number of fully efficient firms	8	9	8	8	9	8	9	9	9	8	8	8
Minimum	0.59056	0.76259	0.75536	0.50447	0.59332	0.85024	0.706	0.726	0.9539	0.1886	0.3058	0.6165
Maximum	1	1	1	1	1	1	1	1	1	1	1	1

Insurer	*FY08*			*FY09*			*FY10*			*FY11*		
	TE	*PTE*	*SE*	*TE*	*PTE*	*SE*	*TE*	*PTE*	*SE*	*TE*	*PTE*	*SE*
Aviva	1	1	1	0.8543	1	0.8543	1	1	1	1	1	1
Bajaj Allianz	1	1	1	1	1	1	1	1	1	1	1	1
Birla Sun Life	0.7138	0.8004	0.8918	1	1	1	0.7091	0.7675	0.9239	0.7104	0.8516	0.8342
HDFC Standard	0.6741	0.8699	0.7749	0.9867	1	0.9867	0.6658	0.7506	0.8870	0.7566	0.9471	0.7988
ICICI Prudential	0.8649	0.8772	0.9860	0.9693	0.9762	0.9929	1	1	1	1	1	1
Exide Life	1	1	1	1	1	1	1	1	1	1	1	1
Kotak Mahindra	1	1	1	1	1	1	1	1	1	1	1	1
Max Life	0.8017	0.8517	0.9413	0.7389	0.8367	0.8831	1	1	1	1	1	1
PNB MetLife	1	1	1	0.8100	0.8242	0.9828	0.5842	0.6365	0.9179	0.9066	1	0.9066
Reliance	0.9037	1	0.9037	0.5694	0.7740	0.7356	0.5981	0.9021	0.6631	0.7293	0.7514	0.9706
SBI Life	0.7701	1	0.7701	0.6900	0.7834	0.8808	1	1	1	1	1	1
TATA AIA	0.5553	0.6417	0.8653	0.5528	0.7819	0.7070	0.5014	0.6481	0.7736	0.4847	0.6718	0.7215
LIC	1	1	1	1	1	1	1	1	1	1	1	1
Memo												
Average	0.868	0.9262	0.9333	0.85935	0.92126	0.92487	0.85066	0.90037	0.9358	0.89136	0.94014	0.94091
SD	0.1525	0.1123	0.0859	0.17101	0.10129	0.10488	0.20195	0.14513	0.10666	0.16762	0.11097	0.09561
Number of fully efficient firms	6	8	6	5	7	5	8	8	8	8	9	8
Minimum	0.5553	0.6417	0.7701	0.55278	0.77401	0.70698	0.50138	0.63647	0.66306	0.48474	0.67182	0.72154
Maximum	1	1	1	1	1	1	1	1	1	1	1	1

Table 2.4 (continued)

Insurer	*FY03*			*FY04*			*FY05*			*FY06*			*FY07*		
	TE	*PTE*	*SE*	*TE*	*PTE*	*SE*	*TE*	*PTE*	*SE*	*TE*	*PTE*	*SE*	*TE*	*PTE*	*SE*
Aviva	0.4783	0.5214	0.9172	0.4414	0.5132	0.8600	0.9370	1	0.9370	0.6657	0.7537	0.8832	0.9401	1	0.9401
Bajaj Allianz	0.7404	0.8462	0.8749	0.7414	0.9997	0.7417	0.6413	1	0.6413	1	1	1	1	1	1
Birla Sun Life	0.3821	0.5239	0.7293	0.2616	0.3105	0.8425	0.4445	0.4984	0.8918	0.4050	0.4070	0.9952	0.3315	0.5313	0.6239
HDFC Standard	0.4093	0.6796	0.6022	0.4882	0.5102	0.9569	0.3537	0.3619	0.9774	0.5232	0.9407	0.5562	0.4908	0.8893	0.5520
ICICI Prudential	0.0824	0.2540	0.3243	0.0790	0.1738	0.4543	0.3609	0.3658	0.9867	0.2698	0.2955	0.9133	0.4838	0.4872	0.9931
Exide Life	1	1	1	1	1	1	1	1	1	0.8344	1	0.8344	0.9722	0.9855	0.9865
Kotak Mahindra	1	1	1	0.8785	1	0.8785	0.8952	1	0.8952	0.7211	0.7353	0.9807	1	1	1
Max Life	0.3265	0.4203	0.7769	0.3574	0.3665	0.9754	0.3347	0.3386	0.9884	0.8806	1	0.8806	1	1	1
PNB MetLife	1	1	1	1	1	1	0.8044	1	0.8044	1	1	1	1	1	1
Reliance	1	1	1	0.8351	1	0.8351	1	1	1	1	1	1	1	1	1
SBI Life	1	1	1	1	1	1	1	1	1	1	1	1	1	1	1
TATA AIA	0.6582	0.7380	0.8918	0.7091	0.7341	0.9659	0.8000	0.8634	0.9266	0.5652	0.7857	0.7193	0.7883	0.8589	0.9178
LIC	1	1	1	1	1	1	1	1	1	1	1	1	1	1	1
Memo															
Average	0.6982	0.768	0.8551	0.6763	0.7391	0.8854	0.7363	0.8022	0.9268	0.7589	0.8398	0.9048	0.8467	0.904	0.9241
SD	0.329	0.2651	0.204	0.3177	0.3191	0.1538	0.2731	0.2899	0.1042	0.2547	0.2406	0.1358	0.2443	0.1815	0.1522
Number of fully efficient firms	6	6	6	4	6	4	4	8	4	5	7	5	7	8	7
Minimum	0.0824	0.254	0.3243	0.079	0.1738	0.4543	0.3347	0.3386	0.6413	0.2698	0.2955	0.5562	0.3315	0.4872	0.552
Maximum	1	1	1	1	1	1	1	1	1	1	1	1	1	1	1

Note: *TE*: Technical Efficiency, *PTE*: Pure Technical Efficiency and *SE*: Scale Efficiency

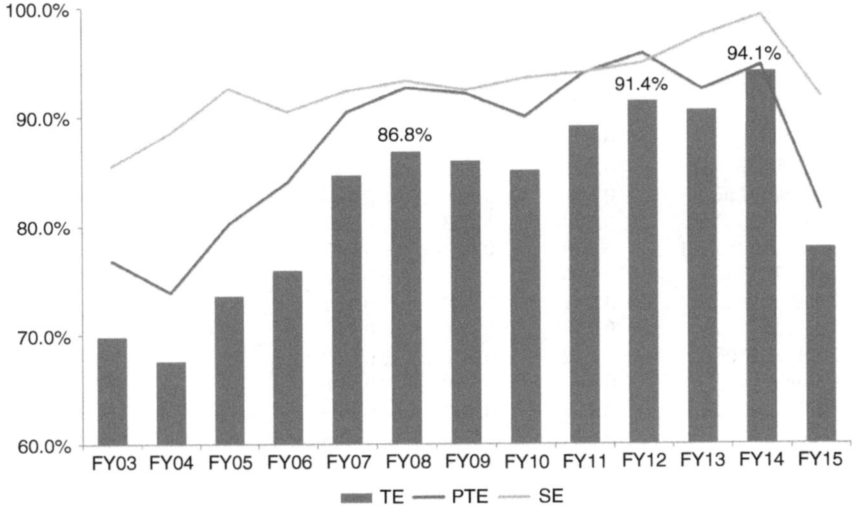

Fig. 2.1 Trends in efficiency of Indian life insurers

Note: *TE*: Technical Efficiency, *PTE*: Pure Technical Efficiency and *SE*: Scale Efficiency

Thus, the TE of the firms has improved due to the new regulations and the increasing competition induced by the gradual liberalization of the sector. However, the average TE score of 81.84% for FY03–15 suggests that life insurance business in India is moderately efficient and hence there is a large room for improvement.

2.4.1.1 Individual Insurer's Mean Efficiency Score

The insurer-wise mean efficiency scores and rank are outlined in Table 2.5 for the period FY03–13. The results indicate that LIC is operating with an efficiency score of 1 and ranked at top, followed by Exide Life and Kotak Mahindra. However, HDFC Life, Birla Sun Life and ICICI Prudential are placed at bottom with ranks of 13, 12 and 11, respectively.

2.4.2 MPI and Its Decomposition

To measure productivity change, the study employs output-oriented MPI approach. In MPI, specification of outputs and inputs is essential. However, the study follows the inputs and outputs (refer Table 2.1)

Table 2.5 Insurer-wise annual average (FY03–15) of TE

Insurers	*Scores*			*Rank*		
	TE	*PTE*	*SE*	*TE*	*PTE*	*SE*
Aviva	0.871	0.907	0.953	8	8	6
Bajaj Allianz	0.933	0.988	0.943	5	3	7
Birla Sun Life	0.560	0.650	0.853	13	13	12
HDFC Standard	0.594	0.743	0.812	12	11	13
ICICI Prudential	0.638	0.672	0.867	11	12	11
Exide Life	0.985	0.999	0.986	2	2	2
Kotak Mahindra	0.961	0.980	0.981	3	5	3
Max Life	0.748	0.796	0.935	9	9	8
PNB MetLife	0.912	0.942	0.967	6	7	5
Reliance	0.885	0.949	0.928	7	6	9
SBI Life	0.958	0.983	0.973	4	4	4
TATA AIA	0.680	0.778	0.868	10	10	10
LIC	1.000	1.000	1.000	1	1	1

Note: *TE*: Technical Efficiency, *PTE*: Pure Technical Efficiency and *SE*: Scale Efficiency

used in the DEA firm efficiency. To estimate the MPI index and its components for the 13 sample insurance firms for the period 2002–2003 to 2014–2015, adopt an output orientation with VRS, which is consistent with our approach in the DEA analysis of firm efficiency. The estimated results of MPI and its components are presented in Tables 2.6–2.8, and insurer-wise mean scores are given in Table 2.9.

- ***Catch-up efficiency scores:*** The catch-up component of the MPI score (Table 2.6) indicates that out of the 13 insurers LIC has scored consistently 1 over the years, implying no change in relative efficiency. However, Bajaj Allianz, which has scored 1.1814 in FY03–04, indicating an 18.14% improvement in relative efficiency from FY03 to FY04, remains steady at 1 after that showing no change in internal efficiency of the insurers. The rest of the 11 private insurer scores showed mixed results but remained steady at 1 in recent years. However, the yearly average score of all 13 insurers indicates that there is consistent improvement in relative efficiency. Further, the catch-up score declined to 0.9705 in FY12–13, indicating a deterioration of internal efficiency by 2.5% from the year FY12 to FY13. Again in FY13–14, average catch up increased to 1.0374, indicating 3.7% growth in internal efficiency,

Table 2.6 Insurer-wise catch-up efficiency scores

Insurers	*FY03–04*	*FY04–05*	*FY05–06*	*FY06– 07*	*FY07–08*	*FY08–09*	*FY09–10*	*FY10–11*	*FY11–12*	*FY12–13*	*FY13–14*	*FY14–15*	*Average*	*Rank*
Aviva	0.9843	1.9484	0.7537	1.3268	1.0000	1.0000	1.0000	1.0000	1.0000	1.0000	1.0000	1.0000	1.0844	3
Bajaj Allianz	1.1814	1.0003	1.0000	1.0000	1.0000	1.0000	1.0000	1.0000	1.0000	1.0000	1.0000	1.0000	1.0151	7
Birla Sun Life	0.5927	1.6050	0.8166	1.3054	1.5065	1.2493	0.7675	1.1096	1.1731	0.5939	1.2237	0.6034	1.0456	5
HDFC Standard	0.7508	0.7093	2.5991	0.9454	0.9783	1.1495	0.7506	1.2617	0.8255	0.8655	1.1433	0.6146	1.0495	4
ICICI Prudential	0.6844	2.1043	0.8078	1.6488	1.8006	1.1128	1.0244	1.0000	1.0000	1.0000	1.0000	0.3058	1.1241	1
Exide Life	1.0000	1.0000	1.0000	0.9855	1.0147	1.0000	1.0000	1.0000	1.0000	1.0000	1.0000	1.0000	1.0000	12
Kotak Mahindra	1.0000	1.0000	0.7353	1.3599	1.0000	1.0000	1.0000	1.0000	1.0000	1.0000	1.0000	1.0000	1.0079	9
Max Life	0.8720	0.9240	2.9532	1.0000	0.8517	0.9824	1.1951	1.0000	1.0000	0.9693	0.8970	0.7936	1.1199	2
PNB MetLife	1.0000	1.0000	1.0000	1.0000	1.0000	0.8242	0.7723	1.5712	1.0000	0.7802	1.2817	1.0000	1.0191	6
Reliance	1.0000	1.0000	1.0000	1.0000	1.0000	0.7740	1.1655	0.8329	1.2133	1.0969	1.0000	1.0000	1.0069	10
SBI Life	1.0000	1.0000	1.0000	1.0000	1.0000	0.7834	1.2765	1.0000	1.0000	1.0000	1.0000	1.0000	1.0050	11
TATA AIA	0.9947	1.1762	0.9100	1.0931	0.7471	1.2185	0.8289	1.0365	1.1351	1.3113	0.9410	0.7365	1.0108	8
LIC	1.0000	1.0000	1.0000	1.0000	1.0000	1.0000	1.0000	1.0000	1.0000	1.0000	1.0000	1.0000	1.0000	13
Average	**0.9277**	**1.1898**	**1.1981**	**1.1281**	**1.0691**	**1.0072**	**0.9831**	**1.0625**	**1.0267**	**0.9705**	**1.0374**	**0.8503**	**1.0376**	–
Max	1.1814	2.1043	2.9532	1.6488	1.8006	1.2493	1.2765	1.5712	1.2133	1.3113	1.2817	1.0000	1.1241	–
Min	0.5927	0.7093	0.7353	0.9454	0.7471	0.7740	0.7506	0.8329	0.8255	0.5939	0.8970	0.3058	1.0000	–
SD	0.1605	0.4221	0.7113	0.2139	0.2772	0.1510	0.1674	0.1792	0.0979	0.1652	0.1102	0.2252	0.0446	–

Table 2.7 Insurer-wise frontier-shift efficiency scores

Insurers	*FY03–04*	*FY04–05*	*FY05–06*	*FY06–07*	*FY07–08*	*FY08–09*	*FY09–10*	*FY10–11*	*FY11–12*	*FY12–13*	*FY13–14*	*FY14–15*	*Average*	*Rank*
Aviva	0.6857	0.4951	0.7063	0.7289	0.9640	1.0000	1.7037	1.0277	1.0643	1.0000	1.0000	1.0000	0.9480	10
Bajaj Allianz	0.5881	0.9998	1.0000	1.0000	1.0000	1.0000	1.0000	1.0000	1.0314	1.2791	1.0000	1.0000	0.9915	7
Birla Sun Life	1.0137	0.9547	0.7194	0.5610	0.7962	0.8336	1.1114	1.0028	1.0666	1.6430	0.9609	1.4023	1.0055	5
HDFC Standard	1.1560	0.9381	0.4027	0.7380	0.8299	0.8556	0.9604	0.9867	1.1444	1.3371	0.9740	2.0551	1.0315	3
ICICI Prudential	1.2000	1.1338	0.9566	0.9051	0.8425	0.8424	2.0846	1.4391	0.8418	1.3893	0.8712	3.6767	1.3486	1
Exide Life	1.0956	0.5889	0.4332	0.7902	0.8962	1.0000	1.0000	1.0000	0.9856	1.2390	0.9821	1.0134	0.9187	13
Kotak Mahindra	0.8077	0.8732	0.9199	0.9076	0.9505	0.8924	1.0000	1.0000	1.0000	1.0000	1.0000	0.9550	0.9422	11
Max Life	0.7955	0.8420	0.6623	0.8136	0.9143	0.8488	0.6925	1.0247	1.1106	1.2584	0.9671	1.1811	0.9259	12
PNB MetLife	0.7835	0.8086	0.9636	0.7346	0.9185	0.8531	0.7486	0.9563	1.1582	1.5969	0.9947	0.9913	0.9590	9
Reliance	0.6496	1.2020	1.1478	0.9323	0.9898	0.7423	0.6405	1.0392	1.0353	1.8613	1.0157	1.2673	1.0436	2
SBI Life	1.0879	1.0000	0.9984	0.7443	0.9746	0.7534	0.9988	1.5111	1.1817	0.7713	0.9974	0.9884	1.0006	6
TATA AIA	0.7754	0.6933	0.7108	0.6376	0.8515	0.7701	0.6295	0.9600	1.1177	1.5812	1.1290	1.6694	0.9605	8
LIC	1.0000	1.0000	1.0000	1.0000	1.0000	1.0000	1.0000	1.0000	1.2268	1.0207	0.9707	1.0000	1.0182	4
Average	**0.8953**	**0.8869**	**0.8170**	**0.8072**	**0.9175**	**0.8763**	**1.0438**	**1.0729**	**1.0742**	**1.3059**	**0.9894**	**1.4000**	**1.0072**	–
Max	1.2000	1.2020	1.1478	1.0000	1.0000	1.0000	2.0846	1.5111	1.2268	1.8613	1.1290	3.6767	1.3486	–
Min	0.5881	0.4951	0.4027	0.5610	0.7962	0.7423	0.6295	0.9563	0.8418	0.7713	0.8712	0.9550	0.9187	–
SD	0.2054	0.2029	0.2304	0.1353	0.0696	0.0960	0.4168	0.1806	0.1004	0.3099	0.0552	0.7591	0.1101	–

Table 2.8 Insurer-wise Malmquist index scores over the period FY03–13

Insurers	*FY03–04*	*FY04–05*	*FY05–06*	*FY06–07*	*FY07–08*	*FY08–09*	*FY09–10*	*FY10–11*	*FY11–12*	*FY12–13*	*FY13–14*	*FY14–15*	*Average*	*Rank*
Aviva	0.6749	0.9646	0.5323	0.9671	0.9640	1.0000	1.7037	1.0277	1.0643	1.0000	1.0000	1.0000	0.9916	7
Bajaj Allianz	0.6948	1.0002	1.0000	1.0000	1.0000	1.0000	1.0000	1.0000	1.0314	1.2791	1.0000	1.0000	1.0005	5
Birla Sun Life	0.6009	1.5323	0.5874	0.7324	1.1996	1.0414	0.8530	1.1127	1.2513	0.9757	1.1758	0.8461	0.9924	6
HDFC Standard	0.8679	0.6655	1.0466	0.6977	0.8119	0.9836	0.7209	1.2449	0.9447	1.1573	1.1137	1.2630	0.9598	11
ICICI Prudential	0.8213	2.3858	0.7728	1.4923	1.5170	0.9374	2.1354	1.4391	0.8418	1.3893	0.8712	1.1245	1.3107	1
Exide Life	1.0956	0.5889	0.4332	0.7787	0.9093	1.0000	1.0000	1.0000	0.9856	1.2390	0.9821	1.0134	0.9188	13
Kotak Mahindra	0.8077	0.8732	0.6764	1.2343	0.9505	0.8924	1.0000	1.0000	1.0000	1.0000	1.0000	0.9550	0.9491	12
Max Life	0.6937	0.7780	1.9559	0.8136	0.7787	0.8338	0.8276	1.0247	1.1106	1.2197	0.8675	0.9373	0.9868	8
PNB MetLife	0.7835	0.8086	0.9636	0.7346	0.9185	0.7031	0.5781	1.5025	1.1582	1.2460	1.2749	0.9913	0.9719	9
Reliance	0.6496	1.2020	1.1478	0.9323	0.9898	0.5745	0.7465	0.8656	1.2562	2.0416	1.0157	1.2673	1.0574	2
SBI Life	1.0879	1.0000	0.9984	0.7443	0.9746	0.5902	1.2749	1.5111	1.1817	0.7713	0.9974	0.9884	1.0100	4
TATA AIA	0.7712	0.8155	0.6469	0.6969	0.6361	0.9384	0.5218	0.9951	1.2687	2.0735	1.0624	1.2295	0.9713	10
LIC	1.0000	1.0000	1.0000	1.0000	1.0000	1.0000	1.0000	1.0000	1.2268	1.0207	0.9707	1.0000	1.0182	3
Average	**0.8115**	**1.0473**	**0.9047**	**0.9095**	**0.9731**	**0.8842**	**1.0278**	**1.1326**	**1.1016**	**1.2626**	**1.0255**	**1.0474**	**1.0106**	–
Max	1.0956	2.3858	1.9559	1.4923	1.5170	1.0414	2.1354	1.5111	1.2687	2.0735	1.2749	1.2673	1.3107	–
Min	0.6009	0.5889	0.4332	0.6969	0.6361	0.5745	0.5218	0.8656	0.8418	0.7713	0.8675	0.8461	0.9188	–
SD	0.1620	0.4685	0.3886	0.2365	0.2109	0.1612	0.4518	0.2180	0.1360	0.3889	0.1120	0.1322	0.0964	–

Table 2.9 Malmquist productivity indices and decomposition: average scores and ranking

Insurers	*Catch up*		*Frontier shift*		*Malmquist index*	
	Average scores[a]	*Rank*	*Average scores*[a]	*Rank*	*Average scores*[a]	*Rank*
Aviva	1.0844	3	0.9480	10	0.9916	7
Bajaj Allianz	1.0151	7	0.9915	7	1.0005	5
Birla Sun Life	1.0456	5	1.0055	5	0.9924	6
HDFC Standard	1.0495	4	1.0315	3	0.9598	11
ICICI Prudential	1.1241	1	1.3486	1	1.3107	1
Exide Life	1.0000	12	0.9187	13	0.9188	13
Kotak Mahindra	1.0079	9	0.9422	11	0.9491	12
Max Life	1.1199	2	0.9259	12	0.9868	8
PNB MetLife	1.0191	6	0.9590	9	0.9719	9
Reliance	1.0069	10	1.0436	2	1.0574	2
SBI Life	1.0050	11	1.0006	6	1.0100	4
TATA AIA	1.0108	8	0.9605	8	0.9713	10
LIC	1.0000	13	1.0182	4	1.0182	3
Average	**1.0376**	–	**1.0072**	–	**1.0106**	–
Max	1.1241	–	1.3486	–	1.3107	–
Min	1.0000	–	0.9187	–	0.9188	–
SD	0.0446	–	0.1101	–	0.0964	–

[a]Average scores of the period FY03–15

while in FY14–15, it declined significantly to 0.8503. The individual insurers' average score for the sample period indicates that all the firms scored more than 1. Among the sample insurers, ICICI Prudential is placed at the top followed by Max Life and Aviva Life in generating internal efficiency but the public-sector giants (LIC: rank 12) and PNB MetLife (rank 13) are placed at the bottom of the efficiency scale.

- ***Frontier-shift efficiency scores:*** The score of frontier-shift component of the MPI is presented in Table 2.7, which indicates that LIC has consistently scored 1.0 up to the year FY11. This means that there is no relative improvement in technology. However, afterwards the scores showed a consistent upward movement in TE by 22.68% and 2.07% from the year FY11 to FY12 and FY12 to FY13, respectively. During FY13–14, though the index declined to 0.9707, there was an improvement in FY15. The private life insurers attained frontier-efficiency scores above 1 only in patches but not on a consistent basis over the years. In the initial years of operation, the private insurers might have been more efficient due to technological innovations. However, the year-wise mean relative frontier-shift scores shows that there is a continuous improvement in the technology.

- ***MPI:*** The change in Malmquist TFP index is the product of catch-up and frontier-shift effects. The insurer-wise MPI (Table 2.8) indicates that LIC has a consistent score of 1 till the year FY10–11, indicating no change in productivity. However, the change in LIC's productivity between years FY11 and FY12 and FY12 and FY13 is due to changes in TE components by 22.68% and 2.07%, respectively. The MPI for the private insurers indicates a mixed result except for HDFC Life, which has been showing continuous improvement in productivity change over the years. The productivity change in HDFC life insurance is due to better performance in both the subcomponents; catch-up and frontier-shift indices.

The individual insurer's mean MPI score in Table 2.9 for the period 2002–2003 to 2014–2015 indicates that ICICI Prudential is placed at the top followed by Reliance, LIC, SBI Life and Bajaj Allianz but Exide Life and Kotak Mahindra are ranked at the bottom of the scale.

There is variation in productivity growth between different periods, ranging from 2.7% in FY09/10 to 26.26% in FY12/13. As far as the source of TFP growth is concerned, one finds efficiency and technical change to be in the same direction in 3 years of the 12-year period, that is, FY03/04, FY10/11 and FY11/12. For all other periods, positive change in one measure is partly offset by negative change in the other, resulting in small or even negative TFP change. The yearly average score of all the 13 insurers shows little improvement in total productivity change over time.

Interestingly, the last line of Table 2.10 indicates that TFP change during the entire period of the FY03–15 period is only 1.0106. This is mainly due to improvement in technical change (catch up) of 1.0375 and TE change (frontier shift) of 1.0072. This result is surprising as a significantly higher increase in TFP and efficiency over time was expected due to deregulation and the consequent intensification of competition in the

Table 2.10 Malmquist index of total factor productivity (average)

Insurers	*Catch up*	*Frontier shift*	*Malmquist index*
FY03–04	0.9277	0.8953	0.8115
FY04–05	1.1898	0.8869	1.0473
FY05–06	1.1981	0.8170	0.9047
FY06–07	1.1281	0.8072	0.9095
FY07–08	1.0691	0.9175	0.9731
FY08–09	1.0072	0.8763	0.8842
FY09–10	0.9831	1.0438	1.0278
FY10–11	1.0625	1.0729	1.1326
FY11–12	1.0267	1.0742	1.1016
FY12–13	0.9705	1.3059	1.2626
FY13–14	1.0374	0.9894	1.0255
FY14–15	0.8503	1.4000	1.0474
FY03–15	1.0375	1.0072	1.0106

Indian life insurance market. It seems that deregulatory efforts have had only a marginal effect on productivity and efficiency in the Indian life insurance.

2.5 Efficiency and Productivity Change

In order to compare the TE score and productivity change, we summarize the values of both TE and its components and MPI and its components in Table 2.11. Interestingly, the table indicates that LIC ranks at number 1 in efficiency change and ranks 13 in catch-up efficiency improvement. However, ICICI Prudential ranks number 1 in productivity change but is placed at 11th position in efficiency change.

2.6 Concluding Remarks

The study employed DEA to calculate the TE, PTE and SE of the sample of 13 insurance companies for the period 2002–2003 to 2014–2015. The DEA score of 1 (0) indicates that the firm is efficient (inefficient). In the second part, to see the productivity change over a period of time, the MPI is calculated. The MPI allows for changes in productivity to be broken down into changes in efficiency (catch-up index) and technological changes (frontier-shift index). If MPI > 1, it indicates a favourable

Table 2.11 Insurer-wise annual average (FY03–15) of efficiency and productivity score

Insurers	*Efficiency change*						*Productivity change*					
	TE		*PTE*		*SE*		*Catch up*		*Frontier shift*		*Malmquist index*	
	Score	*Rank*	*Score*	*Rank*	*Score*	*Rank*	*Scores*	*Rank*	*Score*	*Rank*	*Score*	*Rank*
Aviva	0.8705	8	0.9068	8	0.9532	6	1.0844	3	0.9480	10	0.9916	7
Bajaj Allianz	0.9326	5	0.9881	3	0.9429	7	1.0151	7	0.9915	7	1.0005	5
Birla Sun Life	0.5604	13	0.6498	13	0.8525	12	1.0456	5	1.0055	5	0.9924	6
HDFC Standard	0.5936	12	0.7428	11	0.8124	13	1.0495	4	1.0315	3	0.9598	11
ICICI Prudential	0.6384	11	0.6720	12	0.8667	11	1.1241	1	1.3486	1	1.3107	1
Exide Life	0.9851	2	0.9989	2	0.9862	2	1.0000	12	0.9187	13	0.9188	13
Kotak Mahindra	0.9611	3	0.9796	5	0.9811	3	1.0079	9	0.9422	11	0.9491	12
Max Life	0.7484	9	0.7956	9	0.9352	8	1.1199	2	0.9259	12	0.9868	8
PNB MetLife	0.9121	6	0.9416	7	0.9673	5	1.0191	6	0.9590	9	0.9719	9
Reliance	0.8853	7	0.9492	6	0.9282	9	1.0069	10	1.0436	2	1.0574	2
SBI Life	0.9585	4	0.9833	4	0.9732	4	1.0050	11	1.0006	6	1.0100	4
TATA AIA	0.6801	10	0.7785	10	0.8679	10	1.0108	8	0.9605	8	0.9713	10
LIC	1.0000	1	1.0000	1	1.0000	1	1.0000	13	1.0182	4	1.0182	3

Note: *TE*: Technical Efficiency, *PTE*: Pure Technical Efficiency and *SE*: Scale Efficiency

development, that is, a positive growth in TFP between two periods; MPI < 1 is a negative development, that is, a decline in TFP between two periods; and if MPI = 1, productivity remains unchanged.

The average TE of all 13 life insurance companies in India for FY03 is 69.82% with a minimum score of 25.40% efficiency. However, in FY04 the average declined to 67.63%, with a minimum score of 7.90% with an SD of 31.77%. However, in FY05, the average TE was back to 73.63% with a minimum efficiency score of 33.47% and an SD of 27.31%. After FY05, the average TE scores trended upwards and reached the highest level of 94.12% in FY14, with an SD of 10.36% and a minimum score of 70.60%, which is the highest in the sample period. In FY15, the efficiency index declined to 77.99% as PTE decline significantly. Thus, the TE of the firms has improved due to the new regulations and the increasing competition made by the gradual liberalization of the sector. However, it is also clear that the average TE score for FY03–15 is 81.84%, suggesting that the life insurance business in India is moderately efficient and hence there is a large room for improvement.

The insurer-wise MPI indicates that LIC has consistently scored 1 till the year FY10–11, indicating no change in productivity. However, the change in LIC's productivity between years FY11 and FY12 and FY12 and FY13 is due to the change in TE components by 22.68% and 2.07%, respectively. The MPI for the private insurers indicates a mixed result except for HDFC Life, which has been showing continuous improvement in productivity change over the years. The productivity change in HDFC life insurance is due to better performance in both the subcomponents; catch-up and frontier-shift indices. The individual insurer's mean MPI score for the period 2002–2003 to 2014–2015 indicates that ICICI Prudential is placed at the top followed by Reliance, LIC, SBI Life and Bajaj Allianz but Exide Life and Kotak Mahindra are ranked at the bottom of the scale.

Interestingly, the TFP change over the entire period (FY03–15) is 1.0%. This is contributed by an improvement in technical change (catch up) of 3.7% and TE change (frontier shift) of 0.7%. This result is surprising as a significantly higher increase in TFP and efficiency over time was expected due to deregulation and the consequent intensification of competition in the Indian life insurance market. Therefore, it may be concluded that deregulatory efforts have had a marginal effect on productivity and efficiency of the Indian life insurance industry.

Appendix: Sample of Life Insurance Companies

S. no.	*Insurers*	*Foreign partners*	*Date of registration*	*Year of operation*	*Head office*
1	Life Insurance Corporation of India	–	1.9.1956	1956–1957	Mumbai
2	HDFC Standard Life Insurance Company Ltd.	Standard Life Assurance, UK	23.10.2000	2000–2001	Mumbai
3	Max Life Insurance Company Ltd.	New York Life, USA	15.11.2000	2000–2001	Gurgaon
4	ICICI Prudential Life Insurance Company Ltd.	Prudential Plc, UK	24.11.2000	2000–2001	Mumbai
5	Kotak Mahindra OM Life Insurance Company Ltd.	Old Mutual, South Africa	10.1.2001	2001–2002	Mumbai
6	Birla Sun Life Insurance Company Ltd.	Sun Life, Canada	31.1.2001	2000–2001	Mumbai
7	TATA AIA Life Insurance Company Ltd.	American International Assurance Co., USA	12.2.2001	2001–2002	Mumbai
8	SBI Life Insurance Company Ltd.	BNP Paribas Assurance SA, France	29.3.2001	2001–2002	Mumbai
9	Exide Life Insurance Company Ltd.	–	02.8.2001	2001–2002	Bangalore
10	Bajaj Allianz Life Insurance Company Ltd.	Allianz, Germany	03.8.2001	2001–2002	Pune
11	PNB MetLife India Insurance Company Ltd.	MetLife International Holdings Ltd., USA	06.8.2001	2001–2002	Bangalore
12	Reliance Life Insurance Company Ltd.	–	03.1.2002	2001–2002	Mumbai
13	Aviva Life Insurance Company Ltd.	Aviva International Holdings Ltd., UK	14.5.2002	2002–2003	Gurgaon

References

Banker, R. D., Charnes, A., and Cooper, W. W. (1984), "Some Models for Estimating Technical and Scale Inefficiencies in Data Envelopment Analysis", *Management Science*, Vol. 30, Issue 9, pp. 1078–1092.

Banker, R. D., Chang, H. and Cooper, W. W. (1996), "Equivalence and Implementation of Alternative Methods for Determining Returns to Scale in Data Envelopment Analysis", *European Journal of Operational Research*, Vol. 88, pp. 473–481.

Caves, D. W., Christensen, L. R. and Diewert, W. E. (1982), "The Theory of Index Numbers and Measurement of Input, Output, and Productivity", *Econometrica*, Vol. 50, Issue 6 (Nov 1982), 1393–1414.

Chakraborty, J. and Sengupta, P. P. (2012), "Measuring Performance Growth of the Selected Indian Life Insurance Companies: A Total Factor Productivity Approach", *Arth Prabhand – A Journal of Economics and Management*, Vol. 1 Issue: 6, pp. 2278–2629.

Chakraborty, K., Dutta, A. and Sengupta, P. P. (2012), "Efficiency and Productivity of Indian Life Insurance Industry", *Asia-Pacific Journal of Risk and Insurance*, Vol. 7, Issue 1 (Dec 2012).

Charnes, A., Cooper, W. W. and Rhodes, E. (1978), "Measuring the Efficiency of Decision Making Units", *European Journal of Operational Research*, Volume 2, Issue 6 (Nov 1978), pp. 429–444.

Coelli, T. J., Rao, D. S. P., O'Donnell, C. J. and Battese, G. E. (2005), *An Introduction to Efficiency and Productivity Analysis*, 2nd Edition. New York: Springer Publications, US.

Cooper, W. W., Seiford, L. M. A. and Tone, K. (2007). "*Data Envelopment Analysis: A Comprehensive Text with Models, Applications, References and DEA-Solver Software*", Springer Books, Boston, MA.

Cummins, J. D., Tennyson, S. and Weiss, M. A. (1999), "Consolidation and Efficiency in the US Life Insurance Industry", *Journal of Banking & Finance*, Vol. 23, Issues 2–4, pp. 325–357.

Cummins, J. D. and Misas, M. R. (2006), "Deregulation, Consolidation, and Efficiency: Evidence from the Spanish Insurance Industry", *Journal of Money, Credit and Banking*, Vol. 38, Issue 2, pp. 323–355.

Cummins, J. D. and Xie, X. (2008), "Mergers and acquisitions in the US property-liability insurance industry: Productivity and efficiency effects", *Journal of Banking & Finance*, Vol. 32, pp. 30–55.

Cummins, J. D. and Zi, H. (1998), "Comparison of Frontier Efficiency Methods: An Application to the U.S. Life Insurance Industry", *Journal of Productivity Analysis*, Vol. 10, Issue 2 (Oct 1998), pp. 131–152.

Debreu, G. (1951), "The Coefficient of Resource Utilization", Econometrica, Vol. 19, No. 3 (July 1951), pp. 273–292.

Donni, O., and Fecher, F. (1997), "Efficiency and Productivity of the Insurance Industry in the OECD Countries". *Geneva Papers on Risk and Insurance*, Vol. 22, Issue 84, pp. 523–535.

Dutta A. and Sengupta P. P. (2011), "Efficiency Measurement of Indian Life Insurance Industry in Post-Reforms Era". *Global Business Review*, Vol. 12, No. 3 (October 2011), pp. 415–430.

Eling, M., and Luhnen, M. (2008), "Frontier Efficiency Methodologies to Measure Performance in the Insurance Industry: Overview and New Empirical Evidence", *University of St. Gallen Working Papers on Risk Management and Insurance*, Paper No. 56.

Färe, R., Grosskopf, S., Norris, M., and Zhang, Z. (1994), "Productivity Growth, Technical Progress, and Efficiency Change in Industrialized Countries", *The American Economic Review*, Vol. 84, Issue 1 (Mar 1994), pp. 66–83.

Farrell, M. J. (1957). "The Measurement of Productive Efficiency", *Journal of the Royal Statistical Society*, Series A (General), Vol. 120, Issue 3, pp. 253–290, Blackwell Publishing for the Royal Statistical Society.

Greene, W. H., and Segal, D. (2004), "Profitability and Efficiency in the U.S. Life Insurance Industry", *Journal of Productivity Analysis*, Vol. 21, Issue 3, pp. 229–247, Kluwer Academic Publishers, Netherlands.

Hao, C. J. J., & Chou, L. Y. (2005), "The Estimation of Efficiency for Life Insurance Industry: The Case in Taiwan", *Journal of Asian Economics*, Vol 16, Issue 5, pp. 847–860.

Huang, W. (2007), "Efficiency in the China Insurance Industry, 1999–2004", *Wuhan University, University of Toronto*, pp. 1–29.

Khalid, A. A., Gattoufi, S., & Muharrami, S. A. (2012), "Analyzing the Technical Efficiency of Insurance Companies in GCC", *The Journal of Risk Finance*, Vol. 13, Issue 4, pp. 362–380.

Khan, P. C., and Mitra, D. (2012), "A Study on Technical Efficiency of Life Insurance Companies operating in India in the post Liberalised regime – A Dynamic Panel Approach", Shortlisted Papers for BBAY Award-IV – Insurance Business: Issues & Perspective, *Indian Commerce Association.*

Klopp, G. (1985), "The Analysis of the Efficiency of Production System with Multiple Inputs and Outputs", PhD thesis (University of Illinois at Chicago, Industrial and Systems Engineering College).

Lin, H. D., Lee, Y. H., & Shih, M. L. (2009), "A Study on Technical Efficiency and Productivity Changes of Taiwan's Life Insurance Industry", pp. 1–8, www.jgbm.org/page/10%20Meng-Long%20Shih.pdf.

Nandi, J. K. 2014, "Relative Efficiency Analysis of Selected Life Insurers in India using Data Envelopment Analysis", *Pacific Business Review International*, Vol. 6, Issue 8 (Feb 2014), pp. 69–76.

Noronh, M. R., and Shinde, S. R. (2012), "A Comparative Study of Cost Efficiency of Life Insurance Companies in India", *Ganpat University- Faculty of Management Studies Journal*, 4, (January–June, 2012), pp. 1–14.

Parida, T. K. (2015), "Life Insurance in India: Competition, Efficiency, and Regulation", PhD thesis submitted to and approved by the University of Hyderabad.

Qiu, S., and Chen, B. (2006), "Efficiencies of Life Insurers in China: An Application of DEA", www.cicfconf.org/past/cicf2006/cicf2006paper/20060130033345.pdf.

Rai, A. (1996), "Cost Efficiency of International Insurance Firms", *Journal of Financial Services Research*, Vol. 10, pp. 213–233, (Kluwer Academic Publishers).

Saad, N. M., and Idris, N. E. H. (2011), "Efficiency of Life Insurance Companies in Malaysia and Brunei: A Comparative Analysis", *International Journal of Humanities and Social Science*, Vol. 1, Issue 3, pp. 111–122.

Seiford, L. M. (1997), "A Bibliography for Data Envelopment Analysis (1978–1996)", *Annals of Operations Research*, Vol. 73, October 1997, pp. 393–438.

Sinha, R. P. (2007), "Premium Income of Indian Life Insurance Industry: A Total Factor Productivity Approach", *The IUP Journal of Financial Economics*, Vol. V, Issue 2, pp. 61–69.

Sinha, R. P. (2010), Revenue Maximizing Efficiency of Life Insurance Companies: Some Indian Evidence, *The IUP Journal of Risk & Insurance* Vol. VII, Issue 3 (July 2010), pp. 19–37

Sinha, R. P. and Chatterjee, B. (2009), "Are Indian Life Insurance Companies Cost Efficient?", Conference Proceedings, pp. 1–10, *11th Money & Finance Conference, IGIDR*, http://papers.ssrn.com/sol3/papers.cfm?abstract_id=1391904.

Tone, K. (2002), "A Strange case of the Cost and Allocative Efficiencies in DEA", *Journal of the Operational Research Society*, Vol. 53, Issue 11 (November 2002), pp. 1225–1231.

Tone, K., and Sahoo, B. K. (2005), "Evaluating Cost Efficiency and Returns to Scale in the Life Insurance Corporation of India using Data Envelopment Analysis", *Socio-Economic Planning Sciences*, Vol. 39, Issue 4 (December 2005), pp. 261–285.

Weiss, M. A., and Cummins, J. D. (1991), "Analyzing Firm Performance in the Insurance Industry Using Frontier Efficiency Methods", *The Wharton School Center for Financial Institutions, University of Pennsylvania*, Working Papers No. 98–22.

Yuengert, A. M. (1993), The Measurement of Efficiency in Life Insurance: Estimates of a Mixed Normal-Gamma Error Model, *Journal of Banking & Finance*, Vol. 17, Issue 2 (February 1993), pp. 483–496.

CHAPTER 3

Life Insurance in India: Efficiency and Profitability

Abstract In this chapter, an attempt is made to find out the important factors determining profitability of life insurance companies in India and examine the role of efficiency discussed in the previous chapter. Towards this objective, panel data models are employed to examine the efficiency–profitability relationship. The model employs return on assets as the dependent variable, which is a proxy for profitability of the life insurers and a set of independent variables, including two industry-specific factors like Herfindahl–Hirschman Index (HHI)/CR5 and PE/pure technical efficiency (PTE), three firm-specific variables like 'size', 'leverage' and 'risk' and two macroeconomic factors like 'GDP and inflation'. The data set includes a panel of 13 life insurance companies for the period 2002–2003 to 2014–2015. The panel regression is estimated by both the fixed-effects and random-effects models to find the determinants of profitability. However, Hausman's specification test recommends fixed-effects model to be the appropriate model. The results of fixedeffects model suggest that leverage and size of the firm and two macrovariables, GDP and inflation, are significant determinants of profitability, whereas 'underwriting risk', market structure (HHI/CR5) and efficiency (TE/PTE) are not significant determinants of profitability.

Keywords Profitability · Panel data and market structure and efficiency

T.K. Parida, D. Acharya, *The Life Insurance Industry in India*,
DOI 10.1007/978-981-10-2233-3_3

3.1 Introduction

Profitability is of crucial importance to the life insurance industry, in general (Greene and Segal 2004), and to the deregulated Indian market, in particular. The regulator's eye is on the firm's profitability. To quote Greene and Segal (2004), 'Because of the scrutiny of both net income and equity, the profitability of the insurer determines to large extent its ability to invest and grow.' The external factors beyond the control of management include uncertain macroeconomic environment, regulatory uncertainty, political instability, natural calamities and terrorism, etc. In case of insurance companies, profit not only improves upon insurers' solvency but it also plays an essential role in persuading policyholders and shareholders to supply funds to insurance firms. Thus, one of the objectives of management of insurance companies is to attain profit as an underlying requirement for conducting any insurance business. Without profits no insurer can sustain in the business in the changing and competitive environment.

Since life insurance is a capital-intensive business, global experience of the insurance markets indicates that companies in this sector take about 7/10 years to break-even.[1] However, it has been observed that the Indian life insurers are still facing difficulty in managing their profitability due to a number of factors. For instance, in 2013–2014, out of the 24 life insurers, 18 life insurance companies reported an aggregate loss of Rs. 1,024 crores. The changing environment in the industry merits a fresh look at the factors affecting profitability of the Indian life insurance industry.

The rest of the chapter is organized as follows. Section 3.2 summarizes some of the past empirical studies available with reference to profitability of life insurers and sets the objectives. Section 3.3 presents data and methodology. The empirical results are discussed in Section 3.4. Finally, Section 3.5 offers some concluding remarks.

3.2 Some Past Studies

Given the paucity of studies on this aspect of Indian life insurance, few papers are reviewed in this section in the global context. The review presented is not exhaustive. Greene and Segal (2004) investigate the impact of cost inefficiency on profitability of US life insurance sector and find an inverse relationship between profitability and cost inefficiency in the US life insurance sector. Mok et al. (2007) use a representative sample of the 238 largest foreign-invested toy manufacturing firms in southern China by output value and adopt a two-stage approach to investigate the role of leverage on firm performance as measured by technical efficiency and the effect of technical efficiency on profitability. In the first stage, they employ DEA to estimate technical efficiency of the sample firms. Then they run a regression to study the effects of leverage on efficiency and that of efficiency on profitability. The results support the view that leverage has a positive effect on firm technical efficiency and there is a positive relationship between technical efficiency and profitability. Al-Shami and Hamdan (2008) examine the determinants of profitability using a panel of 25 insurance companies over the period of 2006–2007 listed on UAE stock market. Employing variables such as age of the firm, leverage, volume of capital, risk or loss ratio and firm size, they conclude that firm size has a direct and significant relationship with profitability. Ahmed et al. (2011) investigate the determinants of performance in life insurance sector of Pakistan in a panel of five insurance companies from 2001 to 2007. They explore the relationship between firm-level attributes (leverage, growth, size, age, liquidity, risk and tangibility) and performance of insurance firms. The authors find leverage, size of the firm and risk to be significant determinants of performance. On the other hand, growth, tangibility, age of the firm and liquidity do not have any significant association with performance of life insurance firms. Further, Javaria et al. (2013) examine the determinants of profitability in insurance sector of Pakistan with a panel data set of 31 insurance firms (both life and non-life) for the period 2006–2011. The results indicate leverage, size, earnings volatility and age of the firm to be significant determinants of profitability. Akotey et al. (2013) employ a panel of 10 life insurers over a 10-year period and identify gross premium written, insurer's size, reinsurance, claims, management expenses and interest rate as the significant determinants of life insurer's profitability in Ghana. The results yield gross written premiums to be positively related with insurers' sales profitability and negative with investment income. Also, the study finds that life insurers have been incurring large underwriting losses due to overtrading and price undercutting. A study by Alhassan et al. (2015) examines the market structure, efficiency and profitability of the insurance companies in Ghana using a sample of 14 life and 22 non-life insurers from 2007 to 2011. They employ panel-corrected standard errors (PCSEs) of Beck and Katz (1995) with return on assets (RoA) as the dependent variable, whereas Herfindahl Hirschman Index (HHI) and concentration ratio (four-firm CR) were used as proxies for market structure. Insurers' efficiency is estimated using the DEA technique. Insurer's size, underwriting risk, leverage, GDP growth rate and inflation rate are controlled in the regressions. The results provide ample evidence in support for efficient structure hypothesis for both life and non-life insurance markets. While conflicting results are found for the structure–conduct–performance (SCP) hypothesis in the non-life insurance market, it is rejected in the life insurance market. The findings also point to an increasing level of competition in both life and non-life insurance industries in Ghana.

In the context of Indian insurance industry, the only study to the best of our knowledge, Charumathi (2012) examines the determinants of profitability of the life insurers for the period 2008–2009 to 2010–2011. The author concludes that profitability of life insurers is positively influenced by the size (as explained by logarithm of net premium) and liquidity. The leverage, premium growth and logarithm of equity capital negatively and significantly influence the profitability of Indian life insurers.

3.3 Present Study, Data and Method

In this chapter, an attempt is made to find out the factors determining profitability of life insurance companies in India. The exercise adds to the existing literature in several ways. First, variables such as efficiency and market structure indicators are considered. Secondly, inflation and GDP growth are controlled to account for the effect of macroeconomic environment on insurer's profitability. Finally, the new data series with base year 2004–2005 are considered for macrovariables like GDP and WPI with a longer sample for the insurance companies.

Annual data on insurance indicators are collected from different publications of the IRDAI such as *Annual Reports* (2015) *and Handbook of Indian Insurance Statistics* and *Data Supplement of the Quarterly Journal.* The data on macroeconomic variables, like inflation, savings and GDP, are collected from RBI's database on Indian economy. However, some of the financial indicators of the individual life insurers are collected from the balance sheet of the respective insurers. The data set includes a panel of 13 life insurance companies for the period 2002–2003 to 2014–2015.

3.3.1 Measuring Market Structure

The study employs panel data models to examine the relationship among structure, efficiency and profitability of the life insurance industry. In literature, there are several measures of market structure of an industry, like HHI, CRs (CR_n) and GRS index, etc. In this study, HHI and CR5 are used as a proxy of the market structure of the Indian life insurance industry due to their simplicity and limited data requirements. The estimations on these measures are borrowed from Parida and Acharya (2016). The CR_n and HHI are defined as follows:

- CR_n is defined as the sum of market shares of *n* largest insurer in the market and takes the form: $CR_k = \sum_{i=1}^{k} S_i$, where S_i is the market share of insurer *i* and *k* is the number of insurance companies in concern. ($i = 1, 2, \ldots, k$).
- HHI is defined as the sum of the squares of the relative sizes (expressed as proportions of the total size of the market) of the firms/companies in the market. The formula takes the form: $HHI = \sum_{i=1}^{n} S_i^2$, where S_i stands for the market share of the *i*th company in the industry.

The values of HHI and CR5 are calculated taking into account the 'total premium' of the life insurance companies (Parida and Acharya, 2016; Acharya, 2012), which are given in Table 3.1. The HHI and CR5 indices indicate that the life insurance sector in India is concentrated, though the index is declining considerably due to increasing number of players in the sector.

Table 3.1 Market structure and efficiency (sample insurers' average) of the life insurance industry in India

Year	*Market structure*		*Market efficiency*	
	HHI	*CR5*	*TE*	*PTE*
2002–2003	0.96	0.994	0.698	0.768
2003–2004	0.909	0.984	0.676	0.739
2004–2005	0.823	0.967	0.736	0.802
2005–2006	0.739	0.954	0.759	0.840
2006–2007	0.676	0.941	0.847	0.904
2007–2008	0.563	0.912	0.868	0.926
2008–2009	0.513	0.884	0.859	0.921
2009–2010	0.501	0.871	0.851	0.900
2010–2011	0.496	0.867	0.891	0.940
2011–2012	0.508	0.863	0.914	0.958
2012–2013	0.536	0.874	0.905	0.925
2013–2014	0.574	0.889	0.941	0.947
2014–2015	0.541	0.886	0.780	0.816
Average	0.641	0.914	0.825	0.876

3.3.2 *Measuring Efficiency*

To compute the efficiency of the life insurance companies, DEA technique is employed. The efficiency score of the individual life insurer is calculated by using a set of inputs and outputs. To measure the efficiency of the life insurers, two efficiency scores, that is, technical efficiency (TE) and pure technical efficiency (PTE), are calculated. The efficiency scores estimated under the assumption of CRS are termed as TE (Charnes et al. 1978), which denotes the ability of the firms to employ technology to maximize output. When the input(s) changes result in disproportional changes in the output variable under VRS, it is described as PTE (Banker et al. 1984).

The calculated average efficiency scores of the 13-panel life insurers, using DEA, are given in Table 3.2, which indicates that efficiency (TE and PTE) of the life insurance market has improved over the years.

The individual life insurer's annual average efficiency score for the 13 year (FY03–FY15) is given in Table 3.2. The values above 0.60 indicate that the efficiency of life insurance companies has improved over the years. Further, it is observed that the efficiency score of the individual life insurers varies from 0.08 to 1 in TE and 0.17 to 1 in PTE, indicating that there is significant variation in efficiency among the individual life insurance companies.

Table 3.2 Individual life insurer's annual average (FY03–FY15) of efficiency scores

Insurers	*TE*	*PTE*
Aviva	0.871	0.907
Bajaj Allianz	0.933	0.988
Birla Sun Life	0.560	0.650
HDFC Standard	0.594	0.743
ICICI Prudential	0.638	0.672
Exide Life	0.985	0.999
Kotak Mahindra	0.961	0.980
Max Life	0.748	0.796
PNB MetLife	0.912	0.942
Reliance	0.885	0.949
SBI Life	0.958	0.983
TATA AIA	0.680	0.778
LIC	1.000	1.000

3.3.3 Measuring Profitability

To assess profitability, an attempt is made to find out the important factors determining the profitability of life insurance companies in India. The regression model used in this study is

$$Y_{it} = \alpha_i + \beta_1 \mathrm{MS}_t + \beta_2 \mathrm{ES}_{it} + \sum_{i=1}^{N} \beta_i X_{it} + \sum_{C=1}^{C} \emptyset_c M_t + \mu_{it} \tag{3.1}$$

where Υ_{it} denotes profitability of the insurance company i in a year t, X_{it} represents a vector of variables of an insurer i in year t, M_t is a vector of variables representing the macroeconomic variables in a year t and μ_{it} is the error term.

In our model, RoA is used as a proxy for profitability, which is measured as the ratio of PAT to total assets (TA). As discussed earlier, the market structure (MS) indicators are measured by HHI and CR5, while the efficiency scores (ES) estimated under the DEA technique are TE and PTE. The insure-specific variables, namely 'size', 'leverage' and 'risk', and two macroeconomic variables like 'GDP and inflation' are used as dependent variables in the model. Then Eq. (3.1) can be reformulated as

$$\begin{aligned} \mathrm{RoA}_t = {} & \alpha_i + \beta_1 \mathrm{MP}_t + \beta_2 \mathrm{ES}_{it} + \beta_3 \mathrm{SIZE}_{it} + \beta_4 \mathrm{LEV}_{it} \\ & + \beta_5 \mathrm{RISK}_{it} + \beta_6 \mathrm{GDP}_t + \beta_7 \mathrm{WPI}_t + \mu_{it} \end{aligned} \tag{3.2}$$

A brief description of these variables and their expected relationship are provided in the following:

- *Market structure (MS):* The relationship between 'market structure (MS)' and 'profitability' is expected to be unambiguous as competition may affect the profitability in both ways. If competition increases and efficiency is also increased, then profitability of the life insurers will increase, showing a positive relationship. However, if efficiency does not increase, profitability may reduce due to higher competition in the market.
- *Efficiency (ES):* Efficiency is captured by TE and PTE. Following Mok et al. (2007), a positive relationship between TE and profitability is hypothesized here.
- *Size:* The size of insurance companies is calculated by taking natural logarithm of total assets. It is expected that the relationship between size and profitability is ambiguous. A positive relationship indicates

the benefits of economies of scale, while a negative relationship indicates diseconomies of scale.

- *Leverage:* The leverage of life insurance companies is calculated by the ratio of the total premium to total assets in a year. The relationship is expected to have a mixed result with profitability.
- *Risk:* Insurer's risk is captured by the ratio of benefits paid in a year to total premium collections in that year. This measures the viability of insurance companies in a year. It is hypothesized that the insurers with high underwriting risk would be less profitable; hence, a negative relationship with profitability is expected.
- *GDP growth:* In any financial system, the financial entities like banks, insurance companies, etc., are directly linked with the growth of the economy. Increasing growth stimulates demand for services, which in turn increases the sales of insurance policies and leads to profitability. It is expected that GDP growth would have a positive relationship with profitability through growth in premium collections.
- *Inflation:* In every financial activity, inflation works like a tax on return or interest rate. If inflation increases, RBI would raise the interest rate to keep inflation under control, while the return on investment will increase, due to tight interest rate environment. Hence, it is expected that inflation would have a positive effect on the insurer's profitability. However, a negative relationship can be experienced if the incurred losses exceed gain in investment returns. Additionally, the increase in inflation would reduce the real income, which may put pressure on the sale of policies by insurance companies. So, inflation is expected to have a mixed relationship with profitability.

By including the variables described in Table 3.3, the model (Eq. 3.2) can be expanded into four variants, which we need to estimate to find out the determinants of life insurance companies profitability in India. The models are as follows:

$$\begin{aligned}\mathrm{RoA}_t = {} & \alpha_i + \beta_1\mathrm{HHI}_t + \beta_2\mathrm{TE}_{it} + \beta_3\mathrm{SIZE}_{it} + \beta_4\mathrm{LEV}_{it} \\ & + \beta_5\mathrm{RISK}_{it} + \beta_6\mathrm{GDP}_t + \beta_7\mathrm{WPI}_t + \mu_{it}\end{aligned} \tag{3.3}$$

$$\begin{aligned}\mathrm{RoA}_t = {} & \alpha_i + \beta_1\mathrm{HHI}_t + \beta_2\mathrm{PTE}_{it} + \beta_3\mathrm{SIZE}_{it} + \beta_4\mathrm{LEV}_{it} \\ & + \beta_5\mathrm{RISK}_{it} + \beta_6\mathrm{GDP}_t + \beta_7\mathrm{WPI}_t + \mu_{it}\end{aligned} \tag{3.4}$$

Table 3.3 Choice of variables and hypothesized signs

	Dependent variable	
Return on assets (RoA)	*PAT/TA*	
	Independent variables	
Market structure (MS)	HHI and CR5	+/−
Efficiency (ES)	TE and PTE	+
Size	Ln(total assets)	+/−
Leverage (LEV)	Total premium to total asset ratio	+/−
Risk	Benefits paid to total premium ratio	−
GDP	GDP growth (YoY %)	+
Inflation (WPI)	WPI inflation rate (YoY %)	−

$$\begin{aligned}\text{RoA}_t = {} & \alpha_i + \beta_1\text{CR5}_t + \beta_2\text{PTE}_{it} + \beta_3\text{SIZE}_{it} + \beta_4\text{LEV}_{it} \\ & + \beta_5\text{RISK}_{it} + \beta_6\text{GDP}_t + \beta_7\text{WPI}_t + \mu_{it}\end{aligned} \tag{3.5}$$

$$\begin{aligned}\text{RoA}_t = {} & \alpha_i + \beta_1\text{CR5}_t + \beta_2\text{TE}_{it} + \beta_3\text{SIZE}_{it} + \beta_4\text{LEV}_{it} \\ & + \beta_5\text{RISK}_{it} + \beta_6\text{GDP}_t + \beta_7\text{WPI}_t + \mu_{it}\end{aligned} \tag{3.6}$$

To estimate Eqs. (3.4)–(3.6), linear panel models like fixed-effects (FE) and random-effects (RE) models are estimated.

3.4 Empirical Results and Discussion

3.4.1 Descriptive Statistics

The summary statistics of the variables are presented in Table 3.4. The insurer's profitability, which is a proxy as RoA, indicates on an average a negative value of 4%. While the macroeconomic variables like GDP growth averaged a high growth of 7.61% and inflation rate at 6.26%.

3.4.2 Correlation Matrix

To examine the possibility of high correlation among the independent variables, Pearson's correlation coefficient was estimated and the results

Table 3.4 Descriptive statistics

Variable	*Obs.*	*Mean*	*SD*	*Min*	*Max*
RoA	143	-0.04	0.07	-0.43	0.06
HHI	143	0.66	0.17	0.50	0.96
CR5	143	0.92	0.05	0.86	0.99
TE	143	0.82	0.23	0.08	1.00
PTE	143	0.88	0.20	0.17	1.00
SIZE	143	8.71	2.10	4.57	14.24
LEV	143	0.37	0.17	0.04	0.95
RISK	143	0.22	0.26	0.00	1.43
GDP	143	7.61	1.76	3.90	9.60
WPI	143	6.26	2.00	3.40	9.60

Table 3.5 Correlation matrix

	RoA	*HHI*	*CR5*	*TE*	*PTE*	*SIZE*	*LEV*	*RISK*	*GDP*	*WPI*
RoA	1									
HHI	-0.477	1.000								
CR5	-0.504	0.974	1.000							
TE	0.229	-0.334	-0.328	1.000						
PTE	0.187	-0.339	-0.324	0.931	1.000					
SIZE	0.526	-0.657	-0.561	0.280	0.248	1.000				
LEV	-0.226	0.015	0.157	-0.203	-0.165	-0.267	1.000			
RISK	0.441	-0.479	-0.570	0.366	0.302	0.505	-0.471	1.000		
GDP	0.292	-0.545	-0.518	0.242	0.273	0.374	0.303	0.065	1.000	
WPI	0.285	-0.537	-0.587	0.210	0.205	0.399	-0.131	0.444	0.488	1

are given in Table 3.5. The results confirm that there is no multicollinearity in the models as the values of correlation do not exceed from cut point of 0.5. However, there is a higher correlation between macroeconomic variables with the market structure indicators.

3.4.3 Panel Regression Results

The stated four models in Eqs. (3.4)–(3.6) are estimated by using the FE and RE models of the panel regression, and the results are presented in Table 3.6.

Table 3.6 The panel OLS results: fixed-effects (FE) versus random-effects (RE) models

Dependent variable – RoA								
Regressor	*FE model results*				*RE model results*			
	Model 1	*Model 2*	*Model 3*	*Model 4*	*Model 1*	*Model 2*	*Model 3*	*Model 4*
C	–0.44**	–0.41**	–0.33	–0.38	–0.11	–0.09	0.13	0.10
HHI	0.14	0.13	–	–	–0.05	–0.06	–	–
CR5	–	–	0.11	0.15	–	–	–0.27	–0.26
TE	0.03	–	–	–0.01	–0.01	–	–	–0.01
PTE	–	–0.02	–0.03	–	–	–0.22	–0.02	–
SIZE	0.04**	0.03**	0.02***	0.03***	0.01***	0.01***	0.01***	0.01***
RISK	0.04	0.04	0.05	0.04	0.05***	0.06**	0.05***	0.05***
LEV	–0.09**	–0.09**	–0.09**	–0.09**	–0.08**	–0.08**	–0.07**	–0.07
GDP	0.01**	0.02**	0.01**	0.01**	0.01***	0.01**	0.01**	0.01**
WPI	–0.05***	–0.01***	–0.01	–0.04	–0.01	–0.01	–0.01	–0.01
R^2	Within: 0.4011 Between: 0.2634	Within: 0.4025 Between: 0.2577	Within: 0.3965 Between: 0.2398	Within: 0.3939 Between: 0.2463	Within: 0.3838 Between: 0.2054	Within: 0.3869 Between: 0.1990	Within: 0.3895 Between: 0.1942	Within: 0.3861 Between: 0.2015
F test/ Wald χ^2	11.77	11.84	11.54	11.42	77.19	78.19	79.89	78.85
Prob > F/χ^2	0.0000	0.0000	0.0000	0.0000	0.0000	0.0000	0.0000	0.0000
Hausman test statistic: H_0: RE model is appropriate; H_1: FE model is appropriate								
χ^2	31.21	64.67	10.18	14.46				
Prob. > χ^2	0.0000	0.0000	0.0170	0.0249				

Figures in (#) implies *t*-statistics for FE and *z*-statistics for RE model, Wald χ^2 for RE model
**at 5% level; at 10% level

- Results of FE model: Under the FE model, there are four variables, that is, 'size', 'leverage', 'GDP' and 'WPI', which are significant in all the estimated four models. As expected, both 'size and GDP' coefficients are positive and 'leverage and WPI' coefficients are negative. However, the market structure variables (CR5/HHI) and efficiency variables (TE/PTE) are not significant in the estimated four FE models. The coefficients of the HHI and CR5 are positive, indicating that competition leads to insurer's profitability. However, the TE and PTE coefficients exhibit insignificant mixed results, which do not provide strong evidence for the SCP hypothesis in the life insurance industry in India. The within R^2 in all the four FE model is around 40%, between R^2 is around 25% while overall R^2 is 26%. Within R^2 implies that independent variables explain 40% variations in the profitability in this panel from year to year, that is, 2003–2013. Between R^2 implies that independent variables explain about 25% variations in profitability from firm to firm. Finally, overall R^2 shows that independent variables explain 26% variations in the whole panel. All the estimated four FE models exhibit good fit as evident in the significant *F*.
- RE model results: The results of the four RE models are presented in Table 3.6. In all the four RE models, the variables 'size, risk, leverage and GDP' are significant, while 'CR5/HHI, TE/PTE and WPI' are insignificant. The coefficients of the significant variables 'size, leverage and GDP' are positive, as hypothesized. However, 'risk' was expected to have a negative relationship with profitability but the results show a positive relationship, though the coefficient is very small. The coefficient of WPI is negative as expected, but the variable is insignificant in all the estimated four RE models. The market structure variable (CR5 and HHI) coefficients are negative. Against the expected positive relationship of efficiency (TE and PTE) variable, the estimated results imply a negative relationship with profitability. The models are also significant as its Wald χ^2 is higher and also significant at 1% level. The R^2 of FE models are higher compared to RE models.

To choose the appropriate model, the Hausman (1978) specification test is employed and the results (see Table 3.6) prefer FE to RE. Thus, the FE model in all the estimated four models has four significant variables, 'size, leverage,

GDP and WPI', while the other three variables 'HHI/CR5, TE/PTE and risk' are insignificant. Insurer size is significant, and an important determinant of profitability and positive relationship is found between size and profitability. This implies that bigger life insurance companies are profitable compared to smaller ones, which may be due to better distribution channels, public trust, economies of scale, etc. It is well known that a better economic environment is conducive for the insurance companies for business operation. So, in the estimated models, GDP growth is positively related to profitability. On the other hand, higher inflation leads to higher interest rate environment, which affects the insurance business due to low sales, and thus affects profit of the life insurers. The model expected the efficiency (TE/PTE) of the insurers to lead to better profitability but the estimated values showed mixed results and are insignificant. On the other hand, though, the market structure variables (CR5/HHI) are insignificant but are positively related to profitability of the life insurance companies in India.

3.5 Concluding Remarks

To assess profitability, an attempt is made to find out the important factors determining profitability of life insurance companies in India. Panel data models are employed to examine the relationship among structure, efficiency and performance of the life insurance industry. The model employs RoA as the dependent variable, which is proxy for profitability of the life insurers and a set of independent variables, including two industry-specific factors like HHI/CR5 and PE/PTE, three firm-specific variables like 'size', 'leverage' and 'risk', and two macroeconomic factors like 'GDP and inflation'. The data set includes a panel of 13 life insurance companies for the period 2002–2003 to 2014–2015.

Linear panel models like FE and RE models are estimated. The panel regression is estimated by both the FE and RE models to investigate the determinants of profitability. However, Hausman's (1978) specification test recommends that the FE model is the appropriate model. The results of the FE model suggest that leverage and size of the firm and two macrovariables, GDP and inflation, are significant determinants of profitability while 'underwriting risk', market structure (HHI/CR5) and efficiency (TE/PTE) are not significant determinants of profitability.

To conclude, profitability of the life insurers is positively influenced by the insurer's size (as explained by logarithm of total assets) and leverage (liabilities to assets ratio). Further, the industry-specific factors like market structure (HHI/CR5) also affect the life insurer's profitability with a positive relationship; that is, competition in the industry increases profitability of the life insurers. This study does not find any evidence on the relationship between 'underwriting risk' and 'profitability'. Additionally, macroeconomic variables, GDP and inflation, have a significant positive and negative relationship with profitability of the life insurers in India, respectively.

Now, the question arises that whether competition really results in efficiency and then profitability for the insurers. In economic theory, competition is considered as a positive force to increase efficiency and enhance consumer's welfare. However, the existence of a link between market structure and efficiency was first proposed by Hicks (1935), who argues that monopoly power allows managers a quiet life free from competition and therefore increased concentration should bring about a decrease in efficiency. Leibenstein (1966) claims that inefficiencies are reduced by increasing competition as managers respond to the challenge. Berger and Hannan (1998) relate the impact of market structure on efficiency to several related reasons: (1) high levels of market concentration may allow firms to charge prices in excess of competitive levels and allow manages to benefit from higher prices not necessarily as higher profits but as 'quiet life' (i.e. managers do not need to work hard to keep costs under control); (2) market power may allow managers to pursue objectives other than firm profits; (3) management may use resources to obtain and maintain market power; and (4) the higher prices charged when exploiting market power allow inefficient managers to persist. Berger and Hannan (1998) conclude that market power may allow for managerial incompetence to persist and therefore negatively impact cost efficiency.

In the traditional industrial economics literature, increased market concentration is found to be associated with higher prices and greater than normal profits (Bain 1951). However, a number of banking studies suggest that concentration does not substantially increase bank profitability (Berger 1995). To explain these contradictory findings, Berger and Hannan (1997) argue that banks in more concentrated markets may take advantage of market power in pricing not for earning higher profits but to allow costs to rise as a consequence of slack management. Increased concentration, therefore, has a negative impact on bank efficiency. However, this explanation also implies a lack of market discipline created by market concentration. On the other hand, the efficient structure hypothesis postulates a reverse causality between competition and efficiency. According to the efficient structure hypothesis, more efficient firms have lower costs, which in turn lead to higher profits. Therefore, the most efficient firms are able to increase their market share, resulting in higher concentration.

In the post-reform period, the study found that the level of concentration in the Indian life insurance industry has declined, though the speed of reduction is noticeably slow. In other words, competition in the Indian life insurance industry has increased but at a slower pace. The post 2012–2013 results indicate a rise in concentration due to LIC's gain in market share. Further, efficiency of the life insurers has improved but the average TE score (81.94%) in the post-reform period suggests that life insurance business in India is moderately efficient. Interestingly, the TFP change, measured by MPI, in the said period is negative, –0.05%, which is contributed by an improvement in technical change (catch up) by 5.6% and a decline in TE change (frontier shift) by 3.6%. This result is surprising, as expected a higher TFP, due to deregulation, reduced concentration and moderate efficiency of the Indian life insurance sector in the post-reform period. Further, profitability of the life insurers in India is positively influenced by the insurer's size (as explained by logarithm of total assets) and leverage (liabilities to assets ratio). The market structure, measured by the concentration indices HHI/CR5, is having a significant and positive relationship with profitability. That means an increase in competition implies an increases in profit of the life insurers. While the efficiency, measured by TE and PTE, has a negative relationship with profitability, the results are insignificant.

Thus, in the post-reform period, deregulation of the Indian life insurance sector has intensified competition among the insurers, which has had a positive impact on the insurers' profitability and efficiency. However, there is an inconclusive relationship between the efficiency and profitability of the life insurers.

Note

1. IRDAI Annual Report 2012–2013, page no. 27.

References

Acharya, D. (2012), "Competition in Insurance Sector: Issues and Evidences", *UGC Major Research Project Report*, UGC New Delhi, India.

Ahmed, N., Ahmed, Z., and Usman, A. (2011), "Determinants of Performance: A Case of Life Insurance Sector of Pakistan", *International Research Journal of Finance and Economics*, Vol. 128, Issue 61, 123–128, 2011.

Akotey, J. O., Sackey, F. G., Amoah, L., and Manso, R. F. (2013), "The Financial Performance of Life Insurance Companies in Ghana", *The Journal of Risk Finance*, Vol. 14, Issue 3, pp. 286–302.

Alhassan, A. L., Addisson, G. K. and Asamoah, M. E. (2015), "Market Structure, Efficiency and Profitability of Insurance Companies in Ghana", *International Journal of Emerging Markets*, (2015) Vol. 10, Issue 4, pp. 648–669.

Al-Shami, and Hamdan, A. A. (2008), "Determinants of Insurance Companies Profitability in UAE", *Master's Thesis, Universiti Utara Malaysia*. http://ep3.uum.edu.my/256/

Bain, J. S. (1951), "Relation of Profit Rate to Industry Concentration: American Manufacturing, 1936–1940", *The Quarterly Journal of Economics*, Vol. 65, No. 3 (Aug. 1951), pp. 293–324.

Baltagi, B. H. (2013), *Econometric Analysis of Panel Data*, 5th Edition, Wiley, Chichester, UK.

Banker, R. D., Charnes, A., and Cooper, W. W. (1984), "Some Models for Estimating Technical and Scale Inefficiencies in Data Envelopment Analysis", *Management Science*, Vol. 30, Issue 9, pp. 1078–1092.

Beck, N., and Katz, J. N. (1995), "What to do (and not to do) with Time-Series Cross-Section Data", *The American Political Science Review*, Vol. 89, No. 3 (Sep. 1995), pp. 634–647.

Berger, A. N. (1995), "The Profit-Structure Relationship in Banking – Tests of Market-Power and Efficient Structure Hypotheses", *Journal of Money, Credit, and Banking*, Vol. 27, pp. 404–431.

Berger, A. N., and Hannan, T. H. (1997), "Using Measures of Firm Efficiency to Distinguish among Alternative Explanations of the Structure-Performance Relationships in Banking", *Managerial Finance*, Vol. 23, pp. 6–31.

Berger, A. N., and Hannan, T. H. (1998), "The Efficiency Cost of Market Power in the Banking Industry: A Test of the 'Quiet Life' and Related Hypotheses", *The Review of Economics and Statistics*, Vol. 80, No. 3 (Aug. 1998), pp. 454–465.

Charnes, A., Cooper, W. W., and Rhodes, E. (1978), "Measuring the Efficiency of Decision Making Units", *European Journal of Operational Research*, Vol. 2, Issue 6 (November 1978), pp. 429–444.

Charumathi, B. (2012), "On the Determinants of Profitability of Indian Life Insurers – An Empirical Study", *Proceedings of the World Congress on Engineering 2012*, Vol I, London, U.K.

Greene, W. H., & Segal, D. (2004), "Profitability and efficiency in the US Life Insurance Industry", *Journal of Productivity Analysis*, 21, 3, 229–247.

Hausman, J. A. (1978), Specification Tests in Econometrics, *Econometrica*, Vol. 46, Issue 6, pp. 1251–1271.

Hicks, J. (1935), "The Theory of Monopoly", *Econometrica*, Vol. 3, pp. 1–20.

IRDAI. (2015), "Annual Report of (IRDAI)", 2015 Available: www.IRDAIindia.org.

Javaria, B., Khan, S., and Amjad, T. S. (2013), "Determinants of Profitability Panel Data Evidence from Insurance Sector of Pakistan", *Elixir Financial Management*, Vol. 57A, Issue 2013, pp. 14377–14382.

Leibenstein, H. (1966), "Allocative Efficiency vs. X-Efficiency", *The American Economic Review*, Vol. 56, No. 3, pp. 392–415.

Mok, V., Yeung, G., Han, Z., and Li, Z. (2007), "Leverage, Technical Efficiency and Profitability: An Application of DEA to Foreign-invested Toy Manufacturing Firms in China", *Journal of Contemporary China*, Vol. 16, Issue 51, pp. 259–274.

Parida, T. K., and Acharya, D. (2016), "Competition in Indian Life Insurance Industry: Post Liberalisation Evidence", *International Journal of Business Competition and Growth*, Vol. 5, Nos. 1/2/3, 2016.

CHAPTER 4

Concluding Remarks

Abstract This chapter summarizes and offers some concluding remarks. The brief discussion presents a summary of the findings on efficiency and productivity of the life insurance industry. The main findings on efficiency, and relationship between efficiency and profitability are presented here. The chapter also shares a scepticism on the effects of deregulation on productivity change in the industry.

Keywords Efficiency · Productivity · Profitability and initial public offerings (IPOs)

The insurance industry has a long presence in India but the sector opened up for private and foreign participation in August 2000, that is, after the formation of the IRDAI, with a cap for foreign investment fixed at 26%. With the private and foreign player's participation, the industry structure has moved towards a more competitive market from a pure monopoly. In the post-reform period (2000–2001 to 2014–2015), the insurance sector has recorded an impressive growth, with life insurance business at a CAGR of 17% in total premium and 19% in new business premium collections. There has also been significant expansion of the customer base, product innovations and operational innovations due to increased competition among the players. However, the insurers still grapple with a number of issues, like raising capital, pricing of the product, customer service and

T.K. Parida, D. Acharya, *The Life Insurance Industry in India*,
DOI 10.1007/978-981-10-2233-3_4

profitability. In addition to these sudden regulatory changes, levy of new tax structure and modification in life table, etc., add to the burden of the insurance companies. The companies therefore realign their process and pricing mechanism to remain profitable in the business.

Though the sector has developed in many aspects of insurance compared to the developed countries like the United States, the United Kingdom and France, the Indian life insurance sector still lags in terms of insurance penetration (ratio of premium volume to GDP) and density (ratio of gross premium volume to total population in a country). Life insurance penetration in India was only 2.7% and overall insurance penetration was at 3.4% in 2015. This is indicative of a huge potential for life insurance in India.

To increase the insurance penetration in the country, the government of India has taken a number of steps like increase in FDI limit to 49% from 26%, insurance for public at nominal prices (Jan Suraksha) and health insurance schemes for BPL families, etc. In addition, the IRDAI, the insurance regulator, has allowed insurance companies that have completed 10 years of operations to raise capital through IPOs. Further, to meet the desired capital and bring efficiency in the four public sector non-life insurance companies, in the budget 2016–2017, the government has planned to reduce their stakes by registering in the stock exchanges.

In view of this, the industry merits a review in terms of evolving market structure, efficiency and profitability. An attempt is made in this piece of work to investigate the aspects of competition, efficiency, productivity and profitability for a sample of 13 life insurance companies having consistent operations in all the years of the sample period 2002–2003 to 2014–2015 (13 years). The primary source of data is the IRDAI's (regulator) *Handbook of Indian Insurance Statistics and Public Disclosers of Insurance Companies*, and 2014–2015 is the latest year for which data is available at present. All the life insurance indicators are expressed in real terms by deflating by WPI with base year 2004–2005.

To find out the relative efficiency of the insurer, the study employs DEA to estimate the TE, PTE and SE of the sample of 13 insurance companies for the period 2002–2003 to 2014–2015. The DEA score of 1 (0) indicates that the firm is efficient (inefficient). In the second part, to see the productivity change over a period of time, the MPI is calculated. The MPI allows for changes in productivity to be broken down into changes in efficiency (catch-up index) and technological changes (frontier-shift index). If MPI > 1, it indicates a favourable development, that is, a positive growth in total factor productivity between two periods; MPI < 1 is a negative development, that is, a decline in total factor productivity between two periods, and if MPI equals to 1, productivity remains unchanged.

The average TE of all 13 life insurance companies in India for FY03 is 69.82% with a minimum score of 25.40% efficiency. However, in FY04 the average declined to 67.63%, with a minimum score of 7.90% with an SD of 31.77%. However, in FY05, the average TE was back to 73.63% with a minimum efficiency score of 33.47% and an SD of 27.31%. After FY05, the average TE scores trended upwards and reached the highest level of 94.12% in FY14, with an SD of 10.36% and a minimum score of 70.60%, which is the highest in the sample period. In FY15, the efficiency index declined to 77.99% as PTE declined significantly. Thus, the technical efficiency of the firms has improved due to the new regulations and the increasing competition made by the gradual liberalization of the sector. However, it is also clear that the average TE score for FY03 to FY15 is 81.84%, suggesting that the life insurance business in India is moderately efficient and hence there is a large room for improvement.

The insurer-wise MPI indicates that LIC has consistently scored 1 till the year FY10–11, indicating no change in productivity. However, the change in LIC's productivity between years FY11 and FY12 and FY12 and FY13 is due to the change in TE components by 22.68% and 2.07%, respectively. The MPI for the private insurers indicates a mixed result except for HDFC Life, which has been showing continuous improvement in productivity change over the years. The productivity change in HDFC life insurance is due to better performance in both the subcomponents; catch-up and frontier-shift indices. The individual insurer's mean MPI score for the period 2002–2003 to 2014–2015 indicates that ICICI Prudential is placed at the top followed by Reliance, LIC, SBI Life and Bajaj Allianz but Exide Life and Kotak Mahindra are ranked at the bottom of the scale.

Interestingly, the TFP change over the entire period (FY03–FY15) is negative at 1%. This is contributed by an improvement in technical change (catch up) of 3.7% and technical efficiency change (frontier shift) of 0.7%. This result is surprising as a significantly higher increase in TFP and efficiency over time was expected due to deregulation and the consequent intensification of competition in the Indian life insurance market. Therefore, it can be concluded that deregulatory efforts have had only a marginal effect on productivity and efficiency in the Indian life insurance market.

Further, the study attempts at examining the possible relationship between technical efficiency and profitability controlling for some firm-specific and macroeconomic variables. To conclude, in the post-reform period, deregulation of the Indian life insurance sector has intensified competition among the insurers, which has had a positive impact on the insurers' profitability and efficiency. However, there is an inconclusive relationship between the efficiency and profitability of the life insurers. The results show that deregulatory efforts have had a small effect on productivity change for the life insurance companies in India. It is also seen that in the recent period the monopoly power of LIC is increasing, which may affect the rest of the life insurers, regarding their profitability in short term. So, there is large room for the regulator and government to facilitate competition and efficiency to make the sector sustainable in the long run. Additionally, though India's equity markets are growing in depth and breadth, the insurers need to access the international markets to balance risk and return efficiently.

Going forward, India continues to be a country of savers, though it has witnessed a decline in the household financial saving in the past couple of years. The problem lies in idle household saving or saving instruments that do not help savers achieve their life stage goals. Despite this, the future of the life insurance industry seems to be promising, with several changes in regulatory framework which may lead to further changes in the way the industry conducts its business and engages with its customers. The demographic factors such as growing middle class population, aspirant young generation and increasing awareness of the need for protection and retirement planning ought to support the growth of the Indian life insurance industry. There is also a need for a closer dialogue between the industry and the regulator to ensure more effective and sustainable solution that is in the best interests of ranging from the rural farmer to the urban shareholder.

Kolibri 360 GmbH
Ferdinand-Jühlke-Straße 7
99095 Erfurt, Deutschland
produktsicherheit@kolibri360.de